Getting Started with Angular

Second Edition

Fast-track your web development skills to build high performance SPA with Angular 2 and beyond

Minko Gechev

BIRMINGHAM - MUMBAI

Getting Started with Angular

Second Edition

First published: March 2016

Second edition: February 2017

Production reference: 1210217

Published by Packt Publishing Ltd.
Livery Place
35 Livery Street
Birmingham
B3 2PB, UK.
ISBN 978-1-78712-527-8

www.packtpub.com

Credits

Author

Minko Gechev

Reviewer

Phodal Huang

Acquisition Editor

Shweta Pant

Content Development Editor

Samantha Gonsalves

Technical Editor

Pranav Kukreti

Copy Editor

Dhanya Baburaj

Project Coordinator

Devanshi Doshi

Proofreader

Safis Editing

Indexer

Tejal Daruwale Soni

Graphics

Jason Monteiro

Production Coordinator

Arvindkumar Gupta

Cover Work

Arvindkumar Gupta

Foreword

As a Google Developer Expert for Angular and a frequent blogger and speaker, Minko is well known in the Angular community. Besides being a nice guy, his helpful and technically detailed blog posts have helped many developers to seamlessly transition to the benefits of the latest version of Angular. He is also working on many open source Angular-related projects, such as angular-seed, the Angular style guide, and tools for static analysis of Angular projects.

Published in early 2016 while Angular was still in pre-release, the first edition of *Switching to Angular 2* was one of the earliest books to help developers understand the Angular 2 mind-set. This new version brings the content up to date with the recently released version of Angular, including real-world experience of how this affects production applications.

I'm delighted to see this new update and hope it helps you build amazing things with Angular.

Miško Hevery

January 2017

About the Author

Minko Gechev is a software engineer who strongly believes in open source software. He has developed numerous such projects including codelyzer, the AngularJS style guide, aspect.js and many others. Together with Igor Minar, John Papa and Ward Bell, Minko is one of the coauthors of the official Angular style guide.

Minko loves to experiment with theoretical concepts from computer science and apply them in practice. He has spoken about Angular and software development at worldwide conferences and meetups, including ng-conf, ng-vegas, AngularConnect, FDConf, Angular-SF, and Connect.Tech.

I want to thank Miško Hevery for his great contributions to software engineering and the technical review of this book. He helped me provide as precise content as possible. To make the code samples for this book easy to run, I used angular-seed. One of the core contributors of the project is Ludovic Hénin, who helped make it much more than an Angular starter. I also want to thank Daniel Lamb, Radoslav Kirov, and Tero Parviainen who gave me extremely valuable feedback.

I couldn't have completed this book without the dedicated work of the Packt Publishing team. Finally, I want to thank the team at Google for giving us Angular. They are a constant inspiration.

About the Reviewer

Phodal Huang is a developer, creator, and an author. He works for ThoughtWorks as a consultant now. He currently focuses on IoT and frontend development. He is the author of *Design Internet of Things* and *Growth: Thinking in Full Stack* (in publishing) in Chinese.

He is an open source enthusiast and has created a series of projects in GitHub. After daily work, he likes to reinvent some wheels for fun. He created the application *Growth with Ionic 2 and Angular 2*, which is about coaching newbies how to learn programming. You can find out more wheels in his GitHub page at http://github.com/phodal.

He loves designing, writing, hacking, and traveling; you can also find out more about him through his personal website at http://www.phodal.com.

He has reviewed *Learning Internet of Things* and *Design IoT Projects*.

www.PacktPub.com

For support files and downloads related to your book, please visit www.PacktPub.com.

Did you know that Packt offers eBook versions of every book published, with PDF and ePub files available? You can upgrade to the eBook version at www.PacktPub.com and as a print book customer, you are entitled to a discount on the eBook copy. Get in touch with us at service@packtpub.com for more details.

At www.PacktPub.com, you can also read a collection of free technical articles, sign up for a range of free newsletters and receive exclusive discounts and offers on Packt books and eBooks.

https://www.packtpub.com/mapt

Get the most in-demand software skills with Mapt. Mapt gives you full access to all Packt books and video courses, as well as industry-leading tools to help you plan your personal development and advance your career.

Why subscribe?

- Fully searchable across every book published by Packt
- Copy and paste, print, and bookmark content
- On demand and accessible via a web browser

Customer Feedback

Thanks for purchasing this Packt book. At Packt, quality is at the heart of our editorial process. To help us improve, please leave us an honest review on this book's Amazon page at https://www.amazon.com/dp/1787125270.

If you'd like to join our team of regular reviewers, you can e-mail us at customerreviews@packtpub.com. We award our regular reviewers with free eBooks and videos in exchange for their valuable feedback. Help us be relentless in improving our products!

Table of Contents

Preface

AngularJS is a JavaScript development framework that makes building web applications easier. It is used today in large-scale, high-traffic websites that struggle with performance and portability issues, as well as SEO unfriendliness and complexity at scale. The new version of Angular changes these.

It is the modern framework you need to build performant and robust web applications. *Getting Started with Angular* is the quickest way to get to grips with Angular; it will help you transition into the brave new world of Angular 2 and beyond.

By the end of the book, you'll be ready to start building quick and efficient Angular applications that take advantage of all the new features on offer.

What this book covers

Chapter 1, *Get Going with Angular*, kicks off our journey into the world of Angular. It describes the main reasons behind the design decisions of the framework. We will look at the two main drivers behind the shape of the framework—the current state of the Web and the evolution of frontend development.

Chapter 2, *The Building Blocks of an Angular Application*, gives us an overview of the core concepts introduced by Angular 2. We'll explore how the foundational building blocks for the development of applications provided by AngularJS differ from the ones in the last major version of the framework.

Chapter 3, *TypeScript Crash Course*, explains that although Angular is language agnostic, Google's recommendation is to take advantage of the static typing of TypeScript. In this chapter, you'll learn all the essential syntax you need to know to develop Angular applications in TypeScript.

Chapter 4, *Getting Started with Angular Components and Directives*, describes the core building blocks for developing the user interface of our applications—directives and components. We will dive into concepts such as view encapsulation, content projection, inputs and outputs, change detection strategies, and more. We'll discuss advanced topics, such as template references and speeding up our applications using immutable data.

Chapter 5, *Dependency Injection in Angular*, covers one of the most powerful features in the framework, which was initially introduced by AngularJS: its dependency injection mechanism. It allows us to write more maintainable, testable, and understandable code. By the end of this chapter, we will know how to define the business logic in services and glue them together with the UI through the DI mechanism. We will also look at some more advanced concepts, such as the injectors hierarchy, configuring providers, and more.

Chapter 6, *Working with the Angular Router and Forms*, explores the new module for managing forms in the process of developing a real-life application. We will also implement a page that shows the data entered through the form. In the end, we will glue the individual pages together into an application using the component-based router.

Chapter 7, *Explaining Pipes and Communicating with RESTful Services*, dives into the router and the forms modules in detail. Here, we will explore how we can develop model-driven forms and define parameterized and child routes. We will also explain the HTTP module and take a look at how we can develop pure and impure pipes.

Chapter 8, *Tooling and Development Experience*, explores some advanced topics in the Angular application development, such as Ahead-of-Time compilation, running an application in a Web Worker, and server-side rendering. In the second part of this chapter, we will explore tools that can ease our daily life as developers, such as angular-cli, angular-seed, and more.

What you need for this book

All you need to work through most of the examples in this book is a simple text editor or an IDE, Node.js, an already installed TypeScript, Internet access, and a browser.

Each chapter introduces the software requirements for running the provided snippets.

Who this book is for

Do you want to jump in at the deep end of Angular? Perhaps you're interested in assessing the changes before moving over? If so, then *Getting Started with Angular* is the book for you. To get the most out of the book, you'll need to be familiar with AngularJS and have a good understanding of JavaScript. No knowledge of the changes made to Angular 2 and later versions is required to follow along.

Conventions

In this book, you will find a number of text styles that distinguish between different kinds of information. Here are some examples of these styles and an explanation of their meaning. Code words in text, database table names, folder names, filenames, file extensions, pathnames, dummy URLs, user input, and Twitter handles are shown as follows: "You should see the same result, but without the `test.js` file stored on the disk." A block of code is set as follows:

```
@Injectable()
class Socket {
 constructor(private buffer: Buffer) {}
}

let injector = ReflectiveInjector.resolveAndCreate([
  provide(BUFFER_SIZE, { useValue: 42 }),
  Buffer,
  Socket
]);

injector.get(Socket);
```

When we wish to draw your attention to a particular part of a code block, the relevant lines or items are set in bold:

```
let injector = ReflectiveInjector.resolveAndCreate([
  provide(BUFFER_SIZE, { useValue: 42 }),
  Buffer,
  Socket
]);
```

Each code snippet that is in the repository with the code from this book starts with a comment with its corresponding file location:

```
// ch5/ts/injector-basics/forward-ref.ts

@Injectable()
class Socket {
  constructor(private buffer: Buffer) {...}
}
```

New terms and **important words** are shown in bold. Words that you see on the screen, for example, in menus or dialog boxes, appear in the text surrounded by quotes, or like this: "When the markup is rendered onto the screen, all that the user will see is the label: **Loading....**"

 Warnings or important notes appear in a box like this.

 Tips and tricks appear like this.

Reader feedback

Feedback from our readers is always welcome. Let us know what you think about this book—what you liked or disliked. Reader feedback is important for us, as it helps us develop titles that you will really get the most out of.

To send us general feedback, simply e-mail feedback@packtpub.com, and mention the book's title in the subject of your message.

If there is a topic that you have expertise in and you are interested in either writing or contributing to a book, see our author guide at www.packtpub.com/authors.

Customer support

Now that you are the proud owner of a Packt book, we have a number of things to help you to get the most from your purchase.

Downloading the example code

You can download the example code files for this book from GitHub at https://github.com/mgechev/getting-started-with-angular. You can download the code files by following these steps:

- Enter the URL in your browser's address bar
- Click on the **Download ZIP** button located in the mid-right part of the screen

You can also download the example code files for this book from your account at `http://www.packtpub.com`. If you purchased this book elsewhere, you can visit `http://www.packtpub.com/support` and register to have the files e-mailed directly to you.

You can also download the code files by following these steps:

- Log in or register to our website using your e-mail address and password.
- Hover the mouse pointer on the **SUPPORT** tab at the top.
- Click on **Code Downloads & Errata**.
- Enter the name of the book in the **Search** box.
- Select the book for which you're looking to download the code files.
- Choose from the drop-down menu where you purchased this book from.
- Click on **Code Download**.

Once the file is downloaded, please make sure that you unzip or extract the folder using the latest version of:

- WinRAR / 7-Zip for Windows
- Zipeg / iZip / UnRarX for Mac
- 7-Zip / PeaZip for Linux

Chapters 3 and 4 contain further information for the installation process.

Errata

Although we have taken every care to ensure the accuracy of our content, mistakes do happen. If you find a mistake in one of our books—maybe a mistake in the text or the code—we would be grateful if you could report this to us. By doing so, you can save other readers from frustration and help us improve subsequent versions of this book. If you find any errata, please report them by visiting `http://www.packtpub.com/submit-errata`, selecting your book, clicking on the **Errata Submission Form** link, and entering the details of your errata. Once your errata are verified, your submission will be accepted and the errata will be uploaded to our website or added to any list of existing errata under the Errata section of that title.

To view the previously submitted errata, go to `https://www.packtpub.com/books/content/support` and enter the name of the book in the search field. The required information will appear under the **Errata** section.

Piracy

Piracy of copyrighted material on the Internet is an ongoing problem across all media. At Packt, we take the protection of our copyright and licenses very seriously. If you come across any illegal copies of our works in any form on the Internet, please provide us with the location address or website name immediately so that we can pursue a remedy.

Please contact us at `copyright@packtpub.com` with a link to the suspected pirated material.

We appreciate your help in protecting our authors and our ability to bring you valuable content.

Questions

If you have a problem with any aspect of this book, you can contact us at `questions@packtpub.com`, and we will do our best to address the problem.

1
Get Going with Angular

On September 18, 2014, Google pushed the first public commit to the repository that now contains the new versions of Angular. A few weeks later, at **ng-europe**, Igor and Tobias, from the core team, gave a short overview of what the new version of the framework was expected to be. The vision at that time was far from final; however, one thing was certain: the new version of the framework would be entirely different from AngularJS.

This announcement brought a lot of questions and controversies. The reasons behind the drastic changes were quite clear: AngularJS was no longer able to take full advantage of the evolved Web and the requirements of large-scale JavaScript applications needed to be completely satisfied. A new framework would let Angular developers capitalize on developments in web technology in simpler, more performant, and productive ways. Yet, people were concerned. One of the biggest nightmares with backward incompatibility for developers is the migration of their current codebases to the new version of the third-party software they use. In Angular's case, after that first announcement, migration looked daunting, even impossible. Later, at **ng-conf** 2015 and **ng-vegas** 2015, different migration strategies were introduced. The Angular community came together and shared additional ideas, anticipating the benefits of the new version of the framework, while preserving the things learned from AngularJS.

This book is a part of that project. Making the upgrade to the new versions of Angular is now smooth and is worth it. The main drivers behind the drastic changes in Angular 2 and its lack of backward compatibility are the evolution of the Web and the lessons learned from the usage of AngularJS in the wild. *Getting Started with Angular* will help you learn the new framework by making you understand how we got here and why Angular's new features make intuitive sense for the modern Web in building high-performance, scalable, single-page applications. Some of the topics that we will discuss in this chapter are as follows:

- How to use TypeScript and how it extends JavaScript.

- Building the user interface of Angular applications with a component-based architecture.
- Using Angular's dependency injection mechanism and delegating the business logic to services.
- We are going to explore in-depth Angular's router and forms module.
- We'll take a look at the Ahead-of-Time compilation for building lightning fast applications.

Angular adopted semantic versioning, so before going any further let's have an overview of what this actually means.

Angular and semver

AngularJS was rewritten from scratch and replaced with its successor, Angular 2. A lot of us were bothered by this big step, which didn't allow us to have a smooth transition between these two versions of the framework. Right after Angular 2 was stable, Google announced that they wanted to follow the so called semantic versioning (also known as semver).

Semver defines the version of given software project as the triple **X.Y.Z**, where Z is called **patch version**, Y is called **minor version**, and X is called **major version**. A change in the patch version means that there are no intended breaking changes between two versions of the same project, but only bug fixes. The minor version of a project will be incremented when new functionality is introduced, and there are no breaking changes. Finally, the major version will be increased when incompatible changes are introduced in the API.

This means that between versions 2.3.1 and 2.10.4, there are no introduced breaking changes but only a few added features and bug fixes. However, if we have version 2.10.4 and we want to change any of the already existing public APIs in a backward-incompatible manner (for instance, change the order of the parameters that a method accepts), we need to increment the major version, and reset the patch and minor versions, so we will get version 3.0.0.

The Angular team also follows a strict schedule. According to it, *a new patch version needs to be introduced every week; there should be three monthly minor releases after each major release,* and finally, *one major release every six months.* This means that by the end of 2018, we will have at least Angular 6. However, this doesn't mean that every six months we'll have to go through the same migration path like we did between AngularJS and Angular 2. *Not every major release will introduce breaking changes that are going to impact our projects.* For instance, support for a newer version of TypeScript or change of the last optional argument of a method will be considered as a breaking change. We can think of these breaking changes in a way similar to what happened between AngularJS 1.2 and AngularJS 1.3.

 Since the content that you're going to read in this book will be mostly relevant across different Angular versions, *we'll refer to Angular 2 as either Angular 2 or only Angular*. If we explicitly mention Angular 2, this doesn't mean that the given paragraph will not be valid for Angular 4 or Angular 5; it most likely will. In case you're interested to know what the changes are between different versions of the framework, you can take a look at the changelog at `https://github.com/angular/angular/blob/master/CHAN GELOG.md`. If we're discussing AngularJS (that is, version 1.x of the framework), we will be more explicit by mentioning a version number, or using AngularJS instead of Angular.

Now that we've introduced Angular's semantic versioning and conventions for referring to the different versions of the framework, we can officially start our journey!

The evolution of the Web – time for a new framework

In the past couple of years, the Web has evolved in big steps. During the implementation of ECMAScript 5, the ECMAScript 6 standard started its development (now known as **ECMAScript 2015** or **ES2015**). ES2015 introduced many changes in JavaScript, such as adding built-in language support for modules, block scope variable definition, and a lot of syntactical sugar, such as classes and destructuring.

Meanwhile, **Web Components** were invented. Web Components allow us to define custom HTML elements and attach behavior to them. Since it is hard to extend the existing set of HTML elements with new ones (such as dialogs, charts, grids, and more), mostly because of the time required for consolidation and standardization of their APIs, a better solution is to allow developers to extend the existing elements in the way they want. Web Components provide us with a number of benefits, including better encapsulation, better semantics of the markup we produce, better modularity, and easier communication between developers and designers.

We know that JavaScript is a single-threaded language. Initially, it was developed for simple client-side scripting, but over time, its role has shifted quite a bit. Now, with HTML5, we have different APIs that allow audio and video processing, communication with external services through a two-directional communication channel, transferring and processing big chunks of raw data, and more. All these heavy computations in the main thread may create a poor user experience. They may introduce freezing of the user interface when time-consuming computations are being performed. This led to the development of **Web Workers**, which allow the execution of the scripts in the background that communicate with the main thread through message passing. This way, multithreaded programming was brought to the browser.

Some of these APIs were introduced after the development of AngularJS had begun; that's why the framework wasn't built with most of them in mind. Taking advantage of the APIs gives developers many benefits, such as the following:

- Significant performance improvements.
- Development of software with better quality characteristics.

Now, let's briefly discuss how each of these technologies has been made part of the new Angular core and why.

The evolution of ECMAScript

Nowadays, browser vendors are releasing new features in short iterations, and users receive updates quite often. This helps developers take advantage of bleeding-edge Web technologies. ES2015 is already standardized. The implementation of the latest version of the language has already started in the major browsers. Learning the new syntax and taking advantage of it will not only increase our productivity as developers but will also prepare us for the near future when all browsers will have full support for it. This makes it essential to start using the latest syntax now.

Some projects' requirements may enforce us to support older browsers, which do not support any ES2015 features. In this case, we can directly write ECMAScript 5, which has different syntax but equivalent semantics to ES2015. On the other hand, a better approach will be to take advantage of the process of **transpilation**. Using a transpiler in our build process allows us to take advantage of the new syntax by writing ES2015 and translating it to a target language that is supported by the browsers.

Angular has been around since 2009. Back then, the frontend of most websites was powered by ECMAScript 3, the last main release of ECMAScript before ECMAScript 5. This automatically meant that the language used for the framework's implementation was ECMAScript 3. Taking advantage of the new version of the language requires porting of the entirety of AngularJS to ES2015.

From the beginning, Angular 2 took into account the current state of the Web by bringing the latest syntax in the framework. Although new Angular is written with a superset of ES2016 (TypeScript, which we're going to take a look at in Chapter 3, *TypeScript Crash*

Course), it allows developers to use a language of their own preference. We can use ES2015, or if we prefer not to have any intermediate preprocessing of our code and simplify the build process, we can even use ECMAScript 5. Note that if we use JavaScript for our Angular applications we cannot use **Ahead-of-Time** (**AoT**) compilation. You can find more about AoT compilation in `Chapter 8`, *Tooling and Development Experience*.

Web Components

The first public draft of Web Components was published on May 22, 2012, about three years after the release of AngularJS. As mentioned, the Web Components standard allows us to create custom elements and attach behavior to them. It sounds familiar; we've already used a similar concept in the development of the user interface in AngularJS applications. Web Components sound like an alternative to Angular directives; however, they have a more intuitive API and built-in browser support. They introduced a few other benefits, such as better encapsulation, which is very important, for example, in handling CSS-style collisions.

A possible strategy for adding Web Components support in AngularJS is to change the directives implementation and introduce primitives of the new standard in the DOM compiler. As Angular developers, we know how powerful and complex the directives API is. It includes a lot of properties, such as `postLink`, `preLink`, `compile`, `restrict`, `scope`, `controller`, and much more, and of course, our favorite `transclude`. Approved as standard, Web Components will be implemented on a much lower level in the browsers, which introduces plenty of benefits, such as better performance and native API.

During the implementation of Web Components, a lot of web specialists met with the same problems the Angular team did when developing the directives API, and came up with similar ideas. Good design decisions behind Web Components include the **content** element, which deals with the infamous transclusion problem in AngularJS. Since both the directives API and Web Components solve similar problems in different ways, keeping the directives API on top of Web Components would have been redundant and added unnecessary complexity. That's why the Angular core team decided to start from the beginning by building a framework compatible with Web Components and taking full advantage of the new standard. Web Components involve new features; some of them were not yet implemented by all browsers. In case our application is run in a browser which does not support any of these features natively, Angular emulates them. An example for this is the content element polyfilled with the `ng-content` directive.

Web Workers

JavaScript is known for its event loop. Usually, JavaScript programs are executed in a single thread and different events are scheduled by being pushed in a queue and processed sequentially, in the order of their arrival. However, this computational strategy is not effective when one of the scheduled events requires a lot of computational time. In such cases, the event's handling will block the main thread, and all other events will not be handled until the time-consuming computation is complete and the execution passed to the next one in the queue. A simple example of this is a mouse click that triggers an event, in which callback we do some audio processing using the HTML5 audio API. If the processed audio track is big and the algorithm running over it is heavy, this will affect the user's experience by freezing the UI until the execution is complete.

The Web Workers API was introduced in order to prevent such pitfalls. It allows execution of heavy computations inside the context of a different thread, which leaves the main thread of execution free, capable of handling user input and rendering the user interface.

How can we take advantage of this in Angular? In order to answer this question, let's think about how things work in AngularJS. What if we have an enterprise application, which processes a huge amount of data that needs to be rendered on the screen using data binding? For each binding, the framework will create a new watcher. Once the digest loop is run, it will loop over all the watchers, execute the expressions associated with them, and compare the returned results with the results gained from the previous iteration. We have a few slowdowns here:

- The iteration over a large number of watchers.
- The evaluation of the expression in a given context.
- The copy of the returned result.
- The comparison between the current result of the expression's evaluation and the previous one.

All these steps could be quite slow, depending on the size of the input. If the digest loop involves heavy computations, why not move it to a Web Worker? Why not run the digest loop inside Web Worker, get the changed bindings, and then apply them to the DOM?

There were experiments by the community which aimed for this result. However, their integration into the framework wasn't trivial. One of the main reasons behind the lack of satisfying results was the coupling of the framework with the DOM. Often, inside the watchers' callbacks, AngularJS directly manipulates the DOM, which makes it impossible to move the watchers inside a Web Worker since the Web Workers are executed in an isolated context, without access to the DOM. In AngularJS, we may have implicit or explicit dependencies between the different watchers, which require multiple iterations of the digest loop in order to get stable results. Combining the last two points, it is quite hard to achieve practical results in calculating the changes in threads other than the main thread of execution.

Fixing this in AngularJS introduces a great deal of complexity into the internal implementation. The framework simply was not built with this in mind. Since Web Workers were introduced before the Angular 2 design process started, the core team took them into consideration from the beginning.

Lessons learned from AngularJS in the wild

Although the previous section listed a lot of arguments for the required re-implementation of the framework responding to the latest trends, it's important to remember that we're not starting completely from scratch. We're taking what we've learned from AngularJS with us. In the period since 2009, the Web is not the only thing that evolved. We also started building more and more complex applications. Today, single-page applications are not something exotic, but more like a strict requirement for all web applications solving business problems, which are aiming for high performance and a good user experience.

AngularJS helped us to efficiently build large-scale, single-page applications. However, by applying it in various use cases, we've also discovered some of its pitfalls. Learning from the community's experience, Angular's core team worked on new ideas aiming to answer the new requirements.

Controllers

AngularJS follows the **Model View Controller** (**MVC**) micro-architectural pattern. Some may argue that it looks more like **Model View ViewModel** (**MVVM**) because of the view model attached as properties to the scope or the current context in case of "controller as syntax". It could be approached differently again, if we use the **Model View Presenter pattern** (**MVP**). Because of all the different variations of how we can structure the logic in our applications, the core team called AngularJS a **Model View Whatever** (**MVW**) framework.

The view in any AngularJS application is supposed to be a composition of directives. The directives collaborate together in order to deliver fully functional user interfaces. Services are responsible for encapsulating the business logic of the applications. That's the place where we should put the communication with RESTful services through HTTP, real-time communication with WebSockets, and even WebRTC. Services are the building blocks where we should implement the domain models and business rules of our applications.

There's one more component, which is mostly responsible for handling user input and delegating the execution to the services—the controller.

Although the services and directives have well-defined roles, we can often see the anti-pattern of the **Massive View Controller**, which is common in iOS applications. Occasionally, developers are tempted to access or even manipulate the DOM directly from their controllers. Initially, this happens while you want to achieve something simple, such as changing the size of an element, or quick and dirty changing elements' styles. Another noticeable anti-pattern is the duplication of the business logic across controllers. Often, developers tend to copy and paste logic, which should be encapsulated inside services.

The best practices for building AngularJS applications state that the controllers should not manipulate the DOM at all; instead, all DOM access and manipulations should be isolated in directives. If we have some repetitive logic between controllers, most likely we want to encapsulate it into a service and inject this service with the dependency injection mechanism of Angular in all the controllers that need that functionality.

This is where we're coming from in AngularJS. All this said, it seems that the functionality of controllers could be moved into the directive's controllers. Since directives support the dependency injection API, after receiving the user's input, we can directly delegate the execution to a specific service, already injected. This is the main reason why Angular now uses a different approach, by removing the ability to put controllers everywhere by using the `ng-controller` directive. We'll take a look at how AngularJS controllers' responsibilities could be taken from the new components and directives in Chapter 4, *Getting Started with Angular Components and Directives*.

Scope

Data binding in AngularJS is achieved using the `scope` object. We can attach properties to it and explicitly declare in the template that we want to bind to these properties (one- or two-way). Although the idea of the scope seems clear, it has two more responsibilities, including event dispatching and the change detection-related behavior. Angular beginners have a hard time understanding what scope really is and how it should be used. AngularJS 1.2 introduced something called **controller as syntax**. It allows us to add properties to the current context inside the given controller (`this`), instead of explicitly injecting the `scope` object and later adding properties to it. This simplified syntax can be demonstrated through the following snippet:

```
<div ng-controller="MainCtrl as main">
  <button ng-click="main.clicked()">Click</button>
</div>
```

```
function MainCtrl() {
  this.name = 'Foobar';
}
MainCtrl.prototype.clicked = function () {
  alert('You clicked me!');
};
```

The latest Angular took this even further by removing the `scope` object. All the expressions are evaluated in the context of the given UI component. Removing the entire scope API introduces higher simplicity; we don't need to explicitly inject it anymore, instead we add properties to the UI components to which we can later bind. This API feels much simpler and more natural.

We will take a more detailed look at the components and the change detection mechanism of Angular in `Chapter 4`, *Getting Started with Angular Components and Directives*.

Dependency injection

Maybe the first framework on the market that included **inversion of control** (**IoC**) through **dependency injection** (**DI**) in the JavaScript world was AngularJS. DI provides a number of benefits, such as easier testability, better code organization and modularization, and simplicity. Although the DI in the first version of the framework does an amazing job, Angular 2 took this even further. Since the latest Angular is on top of the latest Web standards, it uses the ECMAScript 2016 decorators' syntax for annotating the code for using DI. Decorators are quite similar to the decorators in Python or annotations in Java. They allow us to *decorate* the behavior of a given object, or add metadata to it, using reflection. Since decorators are not yet standardized and supported by major browsers, their usage requires an intermediate transpilation step; however, if you don't want to take it, you can directly write a little bit more verbose code with ECMAScript 5 syntax and achieve the same semantics.

The new DI is much more flexible and feature-rich. It also fixes some of the pitfalls of AngularJS, such as the different APIs; in the first version of the framework, some objects are injected by position (such as the scope, element, attributes, and controller in the directives' link function) and others, by name (using parameters names in controllers, directives, services, and filters).

We will take a further look at the Angular's dependency injection API in `Chapter 5`, *Dependency Injection in Angular*.

Server-side rendering

The bigger the requirements of the Web are, the more complex web applications become. Building a real-life, single-page application requires writing a huge amount of JavaScript, and including all the required external libraries may increase the size of the scripts on our page to a few megabytes. The initialization of the application may take up to several seconds or even tens of seconds on mobile until all the resources get fetched from the server, the JavaScript is parsed and executed, the page gets rendered, and all the styles are applied. On low-end mobile devices that use a mobile Internet connection, this process may make the users give up on visiting our application. Although there are a few practices that speed up this process, in complex applications, there's no silver bullet.

In the process of trying to improve the user experience, developers discovered something called **server-side rendering**. It allows us to render the requested view of a single-page application on the server and directly provide the HTML for the page to the user. Later, once all the resources are processed, the event listeners and bindings can be added by the script files. This sounds like a good way to boost the performance of our application. One of the pioneers in this was React, which allowed prerendering of the user interface on the server side using Node.js DOM implementations. Unfortunately, the architecture of AngularJS does not allow this. The showstopper is the strong coupling between the framework and the browser APIs, the same issue we had in running the change detection in Web Workers.

Another typical use case for the server-side rendering is for building **Search Engine Optimization** (**SEO**)-friendly applications. There were a couple of hacks used in the past for making the AngularJS applications indexable by the search engines. One such practice, for instance, is the traversal of the application with a headless browser, which executes the scripts on each page and caches the rendered output into HTML files, making it accessible by the search engines.

Although this workaround for building SEO-friendly applications works, server-side rendering solves both of the above-mentioned issues, improving the user experience and allowing us to build SEO-friendly applications much more easily and far more elegantly.

The decoupling of Angular with the DOM allows us to run our Angular applications outside the context of the browser. We will take a further look at it in `Chapter 8`, *Tooling and Development Experience*.

Applications that scale

MVW has been the default choice for building single-page applications since Backbone.js appeared. It allows separation of concerns by isolating the business logic from the view, allowing us to build well-designed applications. Taking advantage of the observer pattern, MVW allows listening for model changes in the view and updating it when changes are detected. However, there are some explicit and implicit dependencies between these event handlers, which make the data flow in our applications not obvious and hard to reason about. In AngularJS, we are allowed to have dependencies between the different watchers, which requires the digest loop to iterate over all of them a couple of times until the expressions' results get stable. The new Angular makes the data flow one-directional; this has a number of benefits:

- More explicit data flow.
- No dependencies between bindings, so no **time to live** (TTL) of the digest.
- Better performance of the framework:
    - The digest loop is run only once.
    - We can create apps, which are friendly to immutable or observable models, that allow us to make further optimizations.

The change in the data flow introduces one more fundamental change in AngularJS architecture.

We may take another perspective on this problem when we need to maintain a large codebase written in JavaScript. Although JavaScript's duck typing makes the language quite flexible, it also makes its analysis and support by IDEs and text editors harder. Refactoring of large projects gets very hard and error-prone because in most cases, the static analysis and type inference are impossible. The lack of compiler makes typos all too easy, which are hard to notice until we run our test suite or run the application.

The Angular core team decided to use TypeScript because of the better tooling possible with it and the compile-time type checking, which help us to be more productive and less error-prone. As the following diagram shows, TypeScript is a superset of ECMAScript; it introduces explicit type annotations and a compiler:

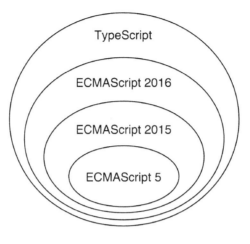

Figure 1

The TypeScript language is compiled to plain JavaScript, supported by today's browsers. Since version 1.6, TypeScript implements the ECMAScript 2016 decorators, which makes it the perfect choice for Angular.

The usage of TypeScript allows much better IDE and text editors' support with static code analysis and type checking. All this increases our productivity dramatically by reducing the mistakes we make and simplifying the refactoring process. Another important benefit of TypeScript is the performance improvement we implicitly get by the static typing, which allows runtime optimizations by the JavaScript virtual machine.

We'll be talking about TypeScript in detail in `Chapter 3`, *TypeScript Crash Course*.

Templates

Templates are one of the key features in AngularJS. They are simple HTML and do not require any intermediate translation, unlike most template engines, such as mustache. Templates in Angular combine simplicity with power by allowing us to extend HTML by creating an internal **domain-specific language** (**DSL**) inside it, with custom elements and attributes.

This is one of the main purposes of Web Components as well. We already mentioned how and why Angular takes advantage of this new technology. Although AngularJS templates are great, they can still get better! The new Angular templates took the best parts of the ones in the previous release of the framework and enhanced them by fixing some of their confusing parts.

For example, let's say we have a directive and we want to allow the user to pass a property to it using an attribute. In AngularJS, we can approach this in the following three different ways:

```
<user name="literal"></user>
<user name="expression"></user>
<user name="{{interpolate}}"></user>
```

In the `user` directive, we pass the `name` property using three different approaches. We can either pass a literal (in this case, the string `"literal"`), a string, which will be evaluated as an expression (in our case `"expression"`), or an expression inside, `{{ }}`. Which syntax should be used completely depends on the directive's implementation, which makes its API tangled and hard to remember.

It is a frustrating task to deal with a large amount of components with different design decisions on a daily basis. By introducing a common convention, we can handle such problems. However, in order to have good results and consistent APIs, the entire community needs to agree with it.

The new Angular deals with this problem by providing special syntax for attributes, whose values need to be evaluated in the context of the current component, and a different syntax for passing literals.

Another thing we're used to, based on our AngularJS experience, is the microsyntax in template directives, such as `ng-if` and `ng-for`. For instance, if we want to iterate over a list of users and display their names in AngularJS, we can use:

```
<div ng-for="user in users">{{user.name}}</div>
```

Although this syntax looks intuitive to us, it allows limited tooling support. However, Angular 2 approached this differently by bringing a little bit more explicit syntax with richer semantics:

```
<template ngFor let-user [ngForOf]="users">
  {{user.name}}
</template>
```

The preceding snippet explicitly defines the property, which has to be created in the context of the current iteration (`user`), and the one we iterate over (`users`).

Since this syntax is too verbose for typing, developers can use the following syntax, which later gets translated to the more verbose one:

```
<li *ngFor="let user of users">
  {{user.name}}
</li>
```

The improvements in the new templates will also allow better tooling for advanced support by text editors and IDEs. We will discuss Angular's templates in `Chapter 4`, *Getting Started with Angular Components and Directives*.

Change detection

In the *Web Workers* section, we already mentioned the opportunity to run the digest loop in the context of a different thread, instantiated as Web Worker. However, the implementation of the digest loop in AngularJS is not quite as memory-efficient and prevents the JavaScript virtual machine from doing further code optimizations, which allows for significant performance improvements. One such optimization is the inline caching (`http://mrale.ph/blog/2012/06/03/explaining-js-vms-in-js-inline-caches.html`).

The Angular team did a lot of research in order to discover different ways the performance and efficiency of the change detection could be improved. This led to the development of a brand new change detection mechanism.

As a result, Angular performs change detection in code that the framework directly generates from the components' templates. The code is generated by the **Angular compiler**. There are two built-in code generation (also known as compilation) strategies:

- **Just-in-Time (JiT) compilation**: At runtime, Angular generates code that performs change detection on the entire application. The generated code is optimized for the JavaScript virtual machine, which provides a great performance boost.
- **Ahead-of-Time (AoT) compilation**: Similar to JiT, with the difference that the code is being generated as part of the application's build process. It can be used for speeding the rendering up by not performing the compilation in the browser and also in environments that disallow `eval()`, such as **CSP** (**Content-Security-Policy**) and Chrome extensions. We will discuss it further in the next sections of the book.

We will take a look at the new change detection mechanisms and how we can configure them in `Chapter 4`, *Getting Started with Angular Components and Directives*.

Summary

In this chapter, we considered the main reasons behind the decisions taken by the Angular core team and the lack of backward compatibility between the last two major versions of the framework. We saw that these decisions were fueled by two things–the evolution of the Web and the evolution of the frontend development, with the lessons learned from the development of AngularJS applications.

In the first section, we learned why we need to use the latest version of the JavaScript language, why to take advantage of Web Components and Web Workers, and why it's not worth it to integrate all these powerful tools in version 1.

We observed the current direction of frontend development and the lessons learned in the last few years. We described why the controller and scope were removed from Angular 2, and why AngularJS's architecture was changed in order to allow server-side rendering for SEO-friendly, high-performance, single-page applications. Another fundamental topic we took a look at was building large-scale applications, and how that motivated single-way data flow in the framework and the choice of the statically typed language, TypeScript.

In the next chapter, we will take a look at the main building blocks of an Angular application, how they can be used and how they relate to each other. The new Angular reuses some of the naming of the concepts introduced by AngularJS, but generally changes the building blocks of our single-page applications completely. We will take a peek at the new concepts and compare them with the ones in the previous version of the framework. We'll make a quick introduction to modules, directives, components, routers, pipes, and services, and describe how they could be combined for building classy, single-page applications.

Downloading the example code

You can download the example code files for this book from your account at `http://www.packtpub.com`. If you purchased this book elsewhere, you can visit `http://www.packtpub.com/support` and register to have the files e-mailed directly to you.

2
The Building Blocks of an Angular Application

In the previous chapter, we looked at the drivers for the design decisions behind the new Angular. We described the main reasons that led to the development of a brand new framework; Angular takes advantage of the newest Web standards while keeping the past lessons in mind. Although we are familiar with the main drivers, we still haven't described the core Angular concepts. The last major release of the framework took a different path from AngularJS and introduced a lot of changes in the fundamental building blocks used for the development of single-page applications.

The mission of this chapter is to describe the framework's core and make a brief introduction to its main concepts. In the next couple of pages, we will also make an overview of how these concepts can be put together to help us build professional user interfaces for our Web applications. The subsequent sections will give us an overview of everything that we will learn in more detail later in this book.

In this chapter, we will take a look at the following topics:

- A conceptual overview of the framework, showing how different concepts relate to each other.
- How we can build a user interface as a composition of components.
- What path the directives took in the new versions of Angular, and how their interface changed compared to the previous major version of the framework.
- The reasons for the enforced separation of concerns, which led to the decomposition of the directives into two different concepts. In order to get a better sense of them, we will demonstrate basic syntax for their definition.
- An overview of the improved change detection, and how it involves the context that directives provide.

- What zones are, and how they can make our daily development process easier.
- What pipes are, and how they are related to the AngularJS filters.
- Introduction to the brand new **dependency injection** (**DI**) mechanism in Angular and how it is related to the services.

A conceptual overview of Angular

Before we dive into the different parts of Angular, let's get a conceptual overview of how everything fits together. Let's take a look at the following diagram:

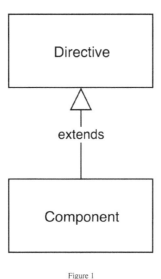

Figure 1

Figure 1 to *Figure 4* show the main Angular concepts and the connections between them. The main purpose of these diagrams is to illustrate the core blocks for building single-page applications with Angular, and their relations.

The **Component** is the main building block we will use to create the user interface of our applications with Angular. The **Component** is a direct successor of the **Directive**, which is the primitive for attaching behavior to the DOM. Components extend **Directives** by providing further features, such as a template, which can be used to render composition of directives. Inside the template of the view can reside different expressions.

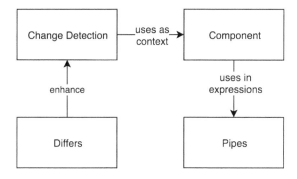

Figure 2

The preceding diagram conceptually illustrates the **Change Detection** mechanism of Angular. It performs dirty checking, which evaluates the registered expressions in the context of specific UI components. Since the concept of scope has been removed from Angular, the execution context of the expressions are the instances of the controllers of the components associated with them.

The **Change Detection** mechanism can be enhanced using **Differs**; that's why there's a direct relation between these two elements on the diagram.

Pipes are another component of Angular. We can think of Pipes as the filters from AngularJS. Pipes can be used together with components. We can include them in the expressions, which are defined in the context of any component.

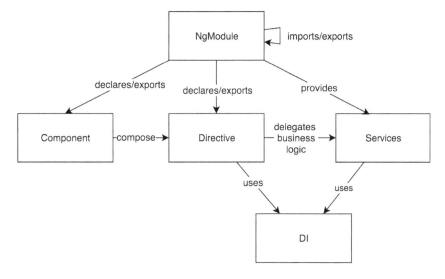

Figure 3

Now let's take a look at the preceding diagram. **Directives** and **Components** delegate the business logic to **Services**. This enforces better separation of concerns, maintainability, and code reusability. **Directives** receive references to instances of specific services declared as dependencies using the **DI** mechanism of the framework, and delegate the execution of the business-related logic to them. Both **Directives** and **Components** may use the **DI** mechanism, not only to inject services but also to inject DOM elements and/or other **Components** or **Directives**.

Modules (also known as **NgModules**) are a core concept which combines the building blocks into separate, logically related, groups. NgModules are quite similar to the AngularJS modules but bring more semantics on top. Note that NgModules are different from the ES2015 modules that we described in Chapter 3, *TypeScript Crash Course*. The Angular modules are a framework feature, in contrast to ES2015 modules which are a language construct.

NgModules have the following responsibilities:

- Provide context of the Angular template compiler.
- Provide a level of encapsulation where we can have components or directives, which are used only within the boundaries of a given module.
- In NgModules, we can configure the providers for the DI mechanism of the framework.

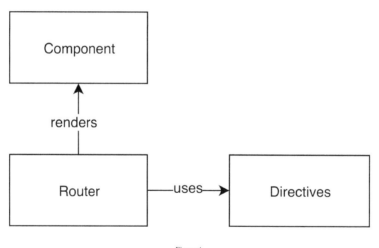

Figure 4

Lastly, the new router is used to define the routes in our application. Since **Directives** do not own a template, only the **Components** can be rendered by the router, representing the different views in our application. The router also uses a set of predefined directives, which allow us to define hyperlinks between the different views and the container where they should be rendered.

Now, we will look more closely at these concepts, see how they work together to make Angular applications, and how they've changed from their AngularJS predecessors.

Changing directives

AngularJS introduced the concept of directives in the development of single-page applications. The purpose of directives is to encapsulate the DOM-related logic and allow us to build user interfaces by composing them. This way, we are able to extend the syntax and the semantics of HTML. Initially, like most innovative concepts, directives were viewed controversially because they predispose us to write invalid HTML when using custom elements or attributes without the `data-` prefix. However, over time, this concept has gradually been accepted and has proved that it is here to stay.

Another drawback of the implementation of directives in AngularJS is the different ways we can use them. This requires an understanding of the attribute values, which can be literals, expressions, callbacks, or microsyntax. This makes tooling essentially impossible.

The latest versions of Angular keep the concept of directives, but take the best parts from AngularJS and add some new ideas and syntax to it. The main purpose of Angular's directives is to attach behavior to the DOM by extending it with custom logic defined in an ES2015 class. We can think of these classes as controllers associated to the directives and think of their constructors as similar to the linking function of the directives from AngularJS. However, the new directives have limited configurability. They do not allow to associate a template with them, which makes most of the already known properties for defining directives unnecessary. The simplicity of the API does not limit directives' behavior, but only enforces stronger separation of concerns. To complement this simpler API, Angular 2 introduced a richer interface for the definition of UI elements, called components. Components extend the functionality of directives by allowing them to own a template, through the **component metadata**. We will take a further look at components later in this book.

The syntax used for Angular directives involves ES2016 decorators. We can use TypeScript, ES2015, or even **ECMAScript 5 (ES5)** in order to achieve the same result with a little bit more typing. This code defines a simple directive, written in TypeScript:

```
@Directive({ selector: '[tooltip]' })
export class Tooltip {
  @Input() tooltip: string;
  private overlay: Overlay;

  constructor(private el: ElementRef, manager: OverlayManager) {
    this.overlay = manager.get();
  }

  @HostListener('mouseenter') onMouseEnter() {
    this.overlay.open(this.el.nativeElement, this.tooltip);
  }

  @HostListener('mouseleave') onMouseLeave() {
    this.overlay.close();
  }
}
```

The directive can be used with the following markup in our template:

```
<div tooltip="42">Tell me the answer!</div>
```

Once the user points over the label, **Tell me the answer!**, Angular will invoke the method defined under the `@HostListener` decorator in the directive's definition. In the end, the `open` method of the overlay manager will be executed.

 Since we can have multiple directives on a single element, the best practices state that we should use an attribute as a selector.

An alternative ECMAScript 5 syntax for the definition of this directive is as follows:

```
var Tooltip = ng.core.Directive({
  selector: '[tooltip]',
  inputs: ['tooltip'],
  host: {
    '(mouseenter)': 'onMouseEnter()',
    '(mouseleave)': 'onMouseLeave()'
  }
})
.Class({
  constructor: [ng.core.ElementRef, Overlay, function (tooltip, el,
```

```
manager) {
    this.el = el;
    this.overlay = manager.get();
  }],
  onMouseEnter() {
    this.overlay.open(this.el.nativeElement, this.tooltip);
  },
  onMouseLeave() {
    this.overlay.close();
  }
});
```

The preceding ES5 syntax demonstrates the internal JavaScript DSL that Angular provides in order to allow us to write our code without the syntax, which is not yet supported by modern browsers.

We can summarize that Angular kept the concept of directives by maintaining the idea of attaching behavior to the DOM. The core differences with AngularJS are the new syntax, and the further separation of concerns introduced by bringing the components. In Chapter 4, *Getting Started with Angular Components and Directives*, we will take a further look at directives' API. We'll also compare the directives' definition syntax using ES2016 and ES5. Now, let's take a look at the big change to Angular components.

Getting to know Angular components

Model View Controller (**MVC**) is a micro-architectural pattern initially introduced for the implementation of user interfaces. As Angular developers, we use different variations of this pattern on a daily basis, most often **Model View ViewModel** (**MVVM**). In MVC, we have the model, which encapsulates the business logic of our application, and the view, which is responsible for rendering the user interface, accepting user input, and delegating the user interaction logic to the controller. The view is represented as composition of components, which is formally known as the **composite design pattern**.

Let's take a look at the following structural diagram, which shows the composite design pattern:

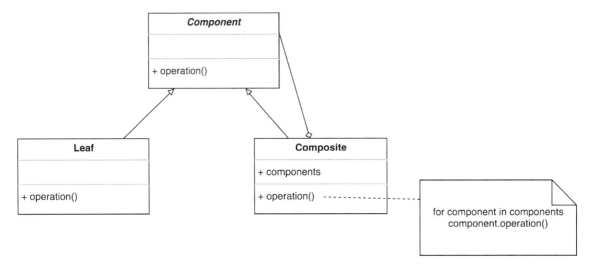

Figure 5

Here, we have three classes:

- An abstract class called `Component`.
- Two concrete classes called `Leaf` and `Composite`. The `Leaf` class is a simple terminal component in the component tree that we will build soon.

The `Component` class defines an abstract operation called `operation`. Both `Leaf` and `Composite` inherit from the `Component` class. However, the `Composite` class also owns references to it. We can take this even further and allow `Composite` to own a list of references to instances of `Component`, as shown in the diagram. The components list inside `Composite` can hold references to different `Composite` or `Leaf` instances, or instances of other classes, which extend the `Component` class or any of its successors. We can have a different behavior of the `operation` methods of the individual `Component` instances invoked within the implementation of the `operation` method of `Composite`. This is because of the late-binding mechanism used for the implementation of polymorphism in object-oriented programming languages.

Components in action

Enough of theory! Let's build a component tree based on the class hierarchy illustrated in the preceding diagram. This way, we will demonstrate how we can take advantage of the composite pattern for building user interface using simplified syntax. We will take a look at a similar example in the context of Angular in `Chapter 4`, *Getting Started with Angular Components and Directives*:

```
Composite c1 = new Composite();
Composite c2 = new Composite();
Composite c3 = new Composite();

c1.components.push(c2);
c1.components.push(c3);

Leaf l1 = new Leaf();
Leaf l2 = new Leaf();
Leaf l3 = new Leaf();

c2.components.push(l1);
c2.components.push(l2);

c3.components.push(l3);
```

The preceding pseudo-code creates three instances of the `Composite` class and three instances of the `Leaf` class. The `c1` instance holds references to `c2` and `c3` inside the components list. The `c2` instance holds references to `l1` and `l2`, and `c3` holds reference to `l3`:

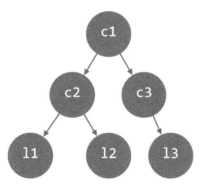

Figure 6

The preceding diagram is a graphical representation of the component tree we built in the snippet. This is a simplified version of what the view in the modern JavaScript frameworks looks similar to. However, it illustrates the very basics of how we can compose directives and components. For instance, in the context of Angular, we can think of directives as instances of the `Leaf` class (since they don't own view and, thus, cannot compose other directives and components) and components as instances of the `Composite` class.

If we think more abstractly for the user interface in AngularJS, we can notice that we used quite a similar approach. The templates of our views compose different directives together in order to deliver a fully functional user interface to the end user of our application.

Components in Angular

Angular took this approach by introducing new building blocks called components. Components extend the directive concept we described in the previous section and provide a broader functionality. Here is the definition of a basic "Hello world" component:

```
@Component({
  selector: 'hello-world',
  template: '<h1>Hello, {{target}}!</h1>'
})
class HelloWorld {
  target: string;
  constructor() {
    this.target = 'world';
  }
}
```

We can use it by inserting the following markup in our view:

```
<hello-world></hello-world>
```

 According to the best practices, we should use a selector of type element for components since we may have only a single component per DOM element.

The alternative ES5 syntax Angular provides using the DSL is as follows:

```
var HelloWorld = ng.core
  .Component({
    selector: 'hello-world',
    template: '<h1>Hello, {{target}}!</h1>'
  })
```

```
.Class({
  constructor: function () {
    this.target = 'world';
  }
});
```

We will take a look at the preceding syntax in more detail later in this book. Now let's briefly describe the functionality that this component provides. Once the Angular application is bootstrapped, it will look at all the elements in the DOM tree and process them. When it finds an element called `hello-world`, it will invoke the logic associated with its definition, which means that the template of the component will be rendered and the expression between the curly brackets will be evaluated. This will result in the markup, `<h1>Hello, world!</h1>`.

So, to summarize, the Angular core team separated out the directives from AngularJS into two different parts–components and directives. Directives provide an easy way to attach behavior to DOM elements without defining a view. Components in Angular provide a powerful, and yet simple-to-learn API, which makes it easier to define the user interface of our applications. Angular components allow us to do the same amazing things as AngularJS directives, but with less typing and fewer things to learn. Components extend the Angular directive concept by adding a view to it. We can think of the relation between Angular components and directives the same way as the relation between `Composite` and `Leaf` from the diagram we saw in *Figure 5*.

Conceptually, we can present the relation between Directive and Component as inheritance. `Chapter 4`, *Getting Started with Angular Components and Directives*, describes these two concepts in further detail.

Angular modules

In AngularJS, we have the concept of modules. Modules there are responsible for grouping pieces of related functionality together and registering it internally during the bootstrap process. Unfortunately, they didn't provide features such as encapsulation and lazy loading.

Angular introduced the NgModules as part of the fifth release candidate of the framework. The main purpose of the new modules is to give a context for the Angular compiler and achieve a good level of encapsulation. For instance, if we are building a library with NgModules, we can have a number of declarations, which are used internally but not exported as part of the public interface. Let's take a look at the following example:

```
import {NgModule} from '@angular/core';
```

```
import {CommonModule} from '@angular/common';
import {TabComponent} from './tab.component';
import {TabItemComponent} from './tab-item.component';

@NgModule({
  imports: [CommonModule],
  declarations: [TabComponent, TabItemComponent],
  exports: [TabComponent]
})
class TabModule { }
```

Do not worry if you're not familiar with the TypeScript syntax in the preceding example; we will take a deep dive into the language in the next chapter.

In the preceding code snippet, using the `@NgModule` decorator, we declare `TabModule`. Note that in the list of `declarations`, we include both `TabComponent` and `TabItemComponent`, but in the list of `exports`, we have only `TabComponent`. This way, we can achieve a level of encapsulation for our library. The users of the module will be able to use only `TabComponent`, so we don't have to worry about backward compatibility of the API of `TabItemComponent` since it's accessible only internally, within the boundaries of our module. Finally, by setting the `imports` property of the object literal passed to `@NgModule`, we can list modules that we want to use inside of the current module. This way, we will be able to take advantage of all the `exports` and `providers` (we'll discuss providers in `Chapter 5`, *Dependency Injection in Angular*) declared by them.

Bootstrapping an Angular application

Similar to AngularJS, before our application gets rendered, it goes through the bootstrap process. In the new Angular, we can bootstrap an application in different ways, depending on the used platform (for instance, web, NativeScript, with JiT or AoT compilation enabled, and so on). Let's take a look at a simple example, of how we can bootstrap a Web app, in order to get a better understanding of how the new Angular modules can be used in the process:

```
import {NgModule} from '@angular/core';
import {platformBrowserDynamic} from '@angular/platform-browser-dynamic';
import {BrowserModule} from '@angular/platform-browser';

import {AppComponent} from './app.component';

@NgModule({
  imports: [BrowserModule],
  bootstrap: [AppComponent],
  declarations: [AppComponent],
```

```
})
export class AppModule {}

platformBrowserDynamic().bootstrapModule(AppModule);
```

In the `@NgModule` decorator in the preceding example, we declare `AppComponent` and we also import `BrowserModule`. Note that this time, we provide value to the `bootstrap` property where we explicitly declare that we want `AppComponent` to be used for bootstrapping our application.

On the last line of the file, we invoke the `bootstrapModule` method of the object returned by the invocation of `platformBrowserDynamic` with argument `AppModule`.

In recap, the modules in Angular have an important role–they not only group the building blocks of our application logically but also provide a way we can achieve encapsulation. Last, but not least, NgModules are heavily used in the application's bootstrap process.

Pipes

In business applications, we often need to have different visual representations of the same piece of data. For example, if we have the number 100,000 and we want to format it as currency, most likely we won't want to display it as plain data; more likely, we'll want something like $100,000.

The responsibility for formatting data in AngularJS was assigned to filters. Another example for a data formatting requirement is when we use collections of items. For instance, if we have a list of items, we may want to filter it based on a predicate (a boolean function); in a list of numbers, we may want to display only the prime numbers. AngularJS has a filter called `filter`, which allows us to do this. However, the duplication of the names often leads to confusion. That's another reason the core team renamed the filter component to a **pipe**.

The motivation behind the new name is the syntax used for pipes and filters:

```
{{expression | decimal | currency}}
```

In the preceding example, we apply the pipes, `decimal`, and `currency`, to the value returned by the `expression`. The entire expression between the curly braces looks like Unix pipe syntax.

Defining pipes

The syntax for defining pipes is similar to the one used for the definition of modules, directives, and components. In order to create a new pipe, we can use the ES2015 decorator, @Pipe. It allows us to add metadata to a class, declaring it as a pipe. All we need to do is provide a name for the pipe and define the data formatting logic. There's also an alternative ES5 syntax, which can be used if we want to skip the process of transpilation.

During runtime, once the Angular expression interpreter finds out that a given expression includes a call of a pipe, it will retrieve it out of the pipes' collection allocated within the component and invoke it with appropriate arguments.

The following example illustrates how we can define a simple pipe called lowercase1, which transforms the given string, passed as argument to its lowercase representation:

```
@Pipe({ name: 'lowercase1' })
class LowerCasePipe1 implements PipeTransform {
  transform(value: string): string {
    if (!value) return value;
    if (typeof value !== 'string') {
      throw new Error('Invalid pipe value', value);
    }
    return value.toLowerCase();
  }
}
```

In order to be consistent, let's show the ECMAScript 5 syntax for defining pipes:

```
var LowercasePipe1 = ng.core
  .Pipe({
    name: 'lowercase1'
  })
  .Class({
    constructor: function () {},
    transform: function (value) {
      if (!value) return value;
      if (typeof value === 'string') {
        throw new Error('Invalid pipe value', value);
      }
      return value.toLowerCase();
    }
  });
```

Using the TypeScript syntax, we implement the `PipeTransform` interface and define the `transform` method declared inside it. However, in ECMAScript 5, we do not have support for interfaces, but we still need to implement the `transform` method in order to define a valid Angular pipe. We will explain the TypeScript interfaces in the next chapter.

Now, let's demonstrate how we can use the `lowercase1` pipe inside a component:

```
@Component({
  selector: 'app',
  template: '<h1>{{"SAMPLE" | lowercase1}}</h1>'
})
class App {}

@NgModule({
  declarations: [App, LowerCasePipe1],
  bootstrap: [App],
  imports: [BrowserModule]
})
class AppModule {}

platformBrowserDynamic().bootstrapModule(AppModule);
```

Also, the alternative ECMAScript 5 syntax for this is as follows:

```
var App = ng.core.Component({
  selector: 'app',
  template: '<h1>{{"SAMPLE" | lowercase1}}</h1>'
})
.Class({
  constructor: function () {}
});

var AppModule = ng.core.NgModule({
  declarations: [App, LowerCasePipe1],
  bootstrap: [App],
  imports: [BrowserModule]
})
.Class({
  constructor: function {}
});

ng.platformBrowserDynamic
  .platformBrowserDynamic()
  .bootstrapModule(AppModule);
```

We can use the `App` component with the following markup:

```
<app></app>
```

The result we will see on the screen is the text sample within an `h1` element. Note that we're including a reference to the `LowerCasePipe1` in the `declarations` property of the `@NgModule` decorator.

By keeping the data formatting logic as a separate component, Angular keeps the strong separation of concerns that can be seen throughout. We will take a look at how we can define stateful and stateless pipes for our application in `Chapter 7`, *Explaining Pipes and Communicating with RESTful Services*.

Improving change detection

As we saw earlier, the view in MVC updates itself, based on change events it receives from the model. A number of **Model View Whatever** (**MVW**) frameworks took this approach and embedded the observer pattern in the core of their change detection mechanism.

Classical change detection

Let's take a look at a simple example, which doesn't use any framework. Suppose, we have a model called `User`, which has a property called `name`:

```
class User extends EventEmitter {
  private name: string;

  setName(name: string) {
    this.name = name;
    this.emit('change');
  }

  getName(): string {
    return this.name;
  }
}
```

The preceding snippet again uses TypeScript. Do not worry if the syntax does not look familiar to you, we will make an introduction to the language in the next chapter.

The `user` class extends the `EventEmitter` class. This provides primitives for emitting and subscribing to events.

Now, let's define a view, which displays the `name` of an instance of the `User` class, passed as an argument to its `constructor`:

```
class View {
  constructor(user: User, el: Element /* a DOM element */) {
    el.innerHTML = user.getName();
  }
}
```

We can initialize the `view` element by:

```
let user = new User();
user.setName('foo');
let view = new View(user, document.getElementById('label'));
```

As the end result, the user will see a label with the content **foo**. However, changes in user will not be reflected by the view. In order to update the view when the `name` of the user changes, we need to subscribe to the `change` event and then update the content of the DOM element. We need to update the `View` definition in the following way:

```
class View {
  constructor(user:User, el:any /* a DOM element */) {
    el.innerHTML = user.getName();
    user.on('change', () => {
      el.innerHTML = user.getName();
    });
  }
}
```

This is how most frameworks used to implement their change detection before the era of AngularJS.

Change detection in AngularJS

Most beginners are fascinated by the data binding mechanism in AngularJS. The basic "Hello world" example looks similar to this:

```
function MainCtrl($scope) {
  $scope.label = 'Hello world!';
}

<body ng-app ng-controller="MainCtrl">
  {{label}}
</body>
```

If you run this, **Hello world!** magically appears on the screen. However, that is not the only most impressive thing! If we add a text input and we bind it to the `label` property of the scope, each change will reflect in the content displayed by the interpolation directive:

```
<body ng-controller="MainCtrl">
  <input ng-model="label">
  {{label}}
</body>
```

How awesome is that! This is one of the main selling points of AngularJS–the extreme ease of achieving data binding. We add a few attributes in our markup, interpolation directive, the `label` property to a mystical object called `$scope`, which is magically passed to a custom function we define, and everything simply works!

The more experienced Angular developer has a better understanding of what is actually going on behind the scenes. In the preceding example, inside the directives, `ng-model` and `ng-bind` (in our case, the interpolation directive, `{{}}`), Angular adds watchers with different behavior associated with the same expression – `label`. These watchers are quite similar to the observers in the classical MVC pattern. On some specific events (in our case, change of the content of the text input), AngularJS will loop over all such watchers, evaluate the expressions associated with them in the context of a given scope, and store their results. This loop is known as the **digest loop**.

In the preceding examples, the evaluation of the expression, `label`, in the context of the scope will return the text, **Hello world!**. On each iteration, AngularJS will compare the current result of the evaluation with the previous result and will invoke the associated callback in case the values differ. For instance, the callback added by the interpolation directive will set the content of the element to be the new result of the expression's evaluation. This is an example of the dependency between the callbacks of the watchers of two directives. The callback of the watcher added by `ng-model` modifies the result of the expression associated with the watcher added by the interpolation directive.

This approach has its own drawbacks. We said that the digest loop will be invoked on some specific events, but what if these events happen outside the framework; for example, what if we use `setTimeout`, and inside the callback, passed as the first argument, we change properties attached to the scope that we're watching? AngularJS will be unaware of the change and won't invoke the digest loop, so we need to do that explicitly using `$scope.$apply`. But, what if the framework knew about all the asynchronous events happening in the browser, such as user events, the `XMLHttpRequest` events, the `WebSocket`-related events, and others? In such a case, Angular would be able to intercept the event's handling and could invoke the digest loop without forcing us to do so!

In the zone.js

That's exactly the case in the new versions of Angular. This functionality is implemented with zones using `zone.js`.

At ng-conf in 2014, Brian Ford gave a talk about zones. Brian presented zones as meta-monkey patching of browser APIs. Zone.js is a library developed by the Angular team, which implements zones in JavaScript. They represent an execution context, which allows us to intercept asynchronous browser calls. Basically, using zones, we are able to invoke a piece of logic just after the given `XMLHttpRequest` completes or when we receive a new `WebSocket` event. Angular took advantage of `zone.js` by intercepting asynchronous browser events and invoking the digest loop just at the right time. This totally eliminates the need for explicit calls of the digest loop by the developer using Angular.

Simplified data flow

The cross-watcher dependencies may create a tangled data flow in our application, which is hard to follow. This may lead to unpredictable behavior and bugs, which are hard to find. Although Angular kept the dirty checking as a way to achieve change detection, it enforced unidirectional data flow. This happened by disallowing dependencies between the different watchers, which allows the digest loop to be run only once. This strategy increases the performance of our applications dramatically and reduces the complexity of the data flow. Angular also made improvements to memory efficiency and the performance of the digest loop. Further details on Angular's change detection and the different strategies used for its implementation can be found in `Chapter 4`, *Getting Started with Angular Components and Directives*.

Enhancing AngularJS's change detection

Now, let's take a step back and again think about the change detection mechanism of the framework.

We said that inside the digest loop, Angular evaluates registered expressions and compares the evaluated values with the values associated with the same expressions in the previous iteration of the loop.

The most optimal algorithm used for the comparison may differ depending on the type of the value returned from the expression's evaluation. For instance, if we get a mutable list of items, we need to loop over the entire collection and compare the items in the collections one by one in order to verify if there is a change or not. However, if we have an immutable list, we can perform a check with a constant complexity, only by comparing references. This is the case because the instances of immutable data structures cannot change. Instead of applying an operation, which intends to modify such instances, we'll get a new reference with the modification applied.

In AngularJS, we can add watchers using a few methods. Two of them are `$watch(exp, fn, deep)` and `$watchCollection(exp, fn)`. These methods give us some level of control over the way the change detection will perform the equality check. For example, adding a watcher using `$watch` and passing a `false` value as a third argument will make AngularJS perform a reference check (that is, compare the current value with the previous one using `===`). However, if we pass a truthy (any `true` value), the check will be deep (that is, using `angular.equals`). This way, depending on the expected type of the return by the expression value, we can add listeners in the most appropriate way in order to allow the framework to perform equality checks with the most optimal algorithm available. This API has two limitations:

- It does not allow you to choose the most appropriate equality check algorithm at runtime.
- It does not allow you to extend the change detection to third parties for their specific data structures.

The Angular core team assigned this responsibility to differs, allowing them to extend the change detection mechanism and optimize it, based on the data we use in our applications. Angular defines two base classes, which we can extend in order to define custom algorithms:

- `KeyValueDiffer`: This allows us to perform advanced diffing over key value-based data structures.
- `IterableDiffer`: This allows us to perform advanced diffing over list-like data structures.

Angular allows us to take full control over the change detection mechanism by extending it with custom algorithms, which wasn't possible in the previous version of the framework. We'll take a further look into the change detection and how we can configure it in `Chapter 4`, *Getting Started with Angular Components and Directives*.

Services

Services are the building blocks that Angular provides for the definition of the business logic of our applications. In AngularJS, we had three different ways of defining services:

```
// The Factory method
```

```
module.factory('ServiceName', function (dep1, dep2, ...) {
  return {
    // public API
  };
});

// The Service method
module.service('ServiceName', function (dep1, dep2, ...) {
  // public API
  this.publicProp = val;
});

// The Provider method
module.provider('ServiceName', function () {
  return {
    $get: function (dep1, dep2, ...) {
      return {
        // public API
      };
    }
  };
});
```

Although the first two syntactical variations provide similar functionality, they differ in the way the registered service will be instantiated. The third syntax allows further configuration of the registered provider during configuration time.

Having three different methods for defining services is quite confusing for the AngularJS beginners. Let's think for a second what necessitated the introduction of these methods for registering services. Why can't we simply use JavaScript constructor functions, object literals, or ES2015 classes instead, which Angular will not be aware of? We could encapsulate our business logic inside a custom JavaScript constructor function like this:

```
function UserTransactions(id) {
  this.userId = id;
}

UserTransactions.prototype.makeTransaction = function (amount) {
  // method logic
};

module.controller('MainCtrl', function () {
  this.submitClick = function () {
    new UserTransactions(this.userId).makeTransaction(this.amount);
  };
});
```

This code is completely valid. However, it doesn't take advantage of one of the key features that AngularJS provides: the DI mechanism. The `MainCtrl` function uses the constructor function, `UserTransaction`, which is visible in its body. The preceding code has two main pitfalls:

- We're coupled with the logic used for the service's instantiation.
- The code is not testable. In order to mock `UserTransactions`, we need to monkey patch it.

How does AngularJS deal with these two things? When a given service is required, through the DI mechanism of the framework, AngularJS resolves all of its dependencies and instantiates it by passing it to a factory function, which encapsulates the logic for its creation. The factory function is passed as the second argument to the `factory` and `service` methods. The `provider` method allows the definition of a service on a lower level; the factory method there is the one under the `$get` property.

Just like AngularJS, the new versions of Angular tolerates this separation of concerns as well, so the core team kept the services. In contrast to AngularJS, the last major version of the framework provides a much simpler interface for their definition by allowing us to use plain ES2015 classes or ES5 constructor functions. We cannot escape from the fact that we need to explicitly state the services that should be available for injection and somehow specify instructions for their instantiation. In contrast to AngularJS, now the framework uses the ES2016 decorator's syntax for this purpose, instead of the methods familiar to us from AngularJS. This allows us to define the services in our applications as simple as ES2015 classes, with decorators for configuration of the DI:

```
import {Injectable} from '@angular/core';

@Injectable()
class HttpService {
  constructor() { /* ... */ }
}

@Injectable()
class User {
  constructor(private service: HttpService) {}

  save() {
    return this.service.post('/users')
      .then(res => {
        this.id = res.id;
        return this;
      });
  }
```

```
}
```

This is the alternative ECMAScript 5 syntax:

```
var HttpService = ng.core.Class({
  constructor: function () {}
});
var User = ng.core.Class({
  constructor: [HttpService, function (service) {
    this.service = service;
  }],
  save: function () {
    return this.service.post('/users')
      .then(function (res) {
        this.id = res.id;
        return this;
      });
  }
});
```

Services are related to the components and the directives described in the previous sections. For developing highly coherent and reusable UI components, we need to move all the business-related logic to inside our services. Also, in order to develop testable components, we need to take advantage of the DI mechanism to resolve all their dependencies.

A core difference with the services in AngularJS is the way their dependencies are being resolved and represented internally. AngularJS uses strings to identify the different services and the associated factories used for their instantiation. On the other hand, now Angular uses keys instead. Usually, the keys are the types of the distinct services. Another core difference in the instantiation is the hierarchical structure of injectors, which encapsulate different dependency providers with different visibility.

Another distinction between the services in the last two major versions of the framework is the simplified syntax. Although the new versions of Angular use ES2015 classes for the definition of our business logic, we can use the ECMAScript 5 `constructor` functions as well or use the DSL provided by the framework. The DI in the latest versions of Angular has a completely different syntax and has improved behavior by providing a consistent way of injecting dependencies. The syntax used in the preceding example uses ES2016 decorators, and in Chapter 5, *Dependency Injection in Angular*, we'll take a look at alternative syntax, which uses ECMAScript 5. You can also find a more detailed explanation of Angular services and DI in Chapter 5, *Dependency Injection in Angular*.

The new router

In traditional Web applications, all the page changes are associated with a full-page reload, which fetches all of the referenced resources and data and renders the entire page onto the screen. However, requirements for Web applications have evolved over time.

Single-page applications (**SPAs**) that we build with Angular simulate desktop user experiences. This often involves incremental loading of the resources and data required by the application, and no full-page reloads after the initial page load. Often, the different pages or views in SPAs are represented by different templates, which are loaded asynchronously and rendered on a specific position on the screen. Later, when the template with all the required resources is loaded and the route is changed, the logic attached to the selected page is invoked and populates the template with data. If the user presses the refresh button after the given page in our SPA is loaded, the same page needs to be re-rendered after the refresh of the view completes. This involves similar behavior: finding the requested view, fetching the required template with all referenced resources, and invoking the logic associated with that view.

The template that needs to be fetched, and the logic that should be invoked after the page reloads successfully, depends on the view selected before the user pressed the refresh button. The framework determines this by parsing the page URL, which contains the identifier of the currently selected page, represented in a hierarchical structure.

All the responsibilities related to the navigation, changing the URL, loading the appropriate template, and invoking specific logic when the view is loaded are assigned to the router component. These are some quite challenging tasks, and support for different navigation APIs required for cross-browser compatibility makes the implementation of routing in modern SPAs a nontrivial problem.

AngularJS introduced the router in its core, which was later externalized into the `ngRoute` module. It allows a declarative way for defining the different views in our SPA, by providing a template for each page and a piece of logic that needs to be invoked when a page is selected. However, the functionality of the router is limited. It does not support essential features, such as nested view routing. That's one of the reasons most developers preferred to use `ui-router`, developed by the community. Both AngularJS's router, and `ui-router`, route-definitions include a route configuration object, which defines a template and a controller associated with the page.

As described in the previous sections, Angular changed the building blocks it provides for the development of SPAs. Angular removes the floating controllers and instead represents views as a composition of components. This necessitates the development of a brand new router, which empowers these new concepts.

The core differences between the AngularJS router and the new Angular router are as follows:

- The new router is component based, `ngRoute` is not. The new Angular router associates a component with the individual routes or a module in case of lazy-loaded routes.
- There is now support for nested views.

Angular route definition syntax

Let's take a brief look at the new syntax used by the Angular router to define routes in our applications:

```
import {Component, NgModule} from '@angular/core';
import {BrowserModule} from '@angular/platform-browser';
import {RouterModule, Routes} from '@angular/router';

import {HomeComponent} from './home/home.component';
import {AboutComponent} from './about/about.component';
import {AppComponent} from './app.component';

const routes: Routes = [
  { path: 'home', component: HomeComponent },
  { path: 'about', component: AboutComponent }
];

@NgModule({
  imports: [BrowserModule, RouterModule.forRoot(routes)],
  declarations: [AppComponent, HomeComponent, AboutComponent],
  bootstrap: [AppComponent]
})
export class AppModule {}
```

We won't go into too much detail here since Chapter 6, *Working with the Angular Router and Forms*, and Chapter 7, *Explaining Pipes and Communicating with RESTful Services*, are dedicated to the new router, but let's mention the main points in the preceding code snippet.

The router lives in `@angular/router`. Since `AppModule` is the root module of our application, we use the `forRoot` method of `RouterModule` in order to import all the required directives and services exported by the router.

The parameter passed to the `RouterModule.forRoot` decorator shows how we define the routes in our application. We use an array with objects, which defines the mappings between routes and the components associated with them.

Summary

In this chapter, we took a quick overview of the main building blocks for developing SPAs provided by Angular. We pointed out the main differences with the core concepts from AngularJS.

Although we can use ES2015, or even ES5, to build Angular applications, the recommendation from Google is to take advantage of the language used for the development of the framework–TypeScript. This way we can use advanced features such as Ahead-of-Time compilation that we're going to describe in `Chapter 8`, *Tooling and Development Experience*.

In the next chapter, we'll take a look at TypeScript and how we can start using it in our next application. We will also explain how with ambient type definitions we can take advantage of the static typing in the JavaScript libraries and frameworks written in vanilla JavaScript.

3
TypeScript Crash Course

In this chapter, we will start working with TypeScript, the language Google recommends for using with Angular. All the features ECMAScript 2015 and ECMAScript 2016 provide, such as functions, classes, modules, and decorators, are already implemented in or added to the roadmap of TypeScript. Because of the extra type annotations, there are some syntactical additions compared to JavaScript.

For a smoother transition from the language which is fully supported by modern browsers at the time of writing, that is, ES5, we will start with some common features between ES2016 and TypeScript. Where there are differences between the ES2016 syntax and TypeScript, we'll explicitly mention it. In the second half of the chapter, we'll add the type annotations to everything we've learned until this point.

Later in this chapter, we will explain the extra features TypeScript provides, such as static typing and extra syntax. We will discuss the different consequences based on these features, which will help us to be more productive and less error-prone. Let's get going!

Introduction to TypeScript

TypeScript is an open source programming language that is developed and maintained by Microsoft. Its initial public release was in October 2012. TypeScript is a superset of ECMAScript, supporting all of the syntax and semantics of JavaScript with some extra features on top, such as static typing and richer syntax.

Figure 1 shows the relationships among ES5, ES2015, ES2016, and TypeScript.

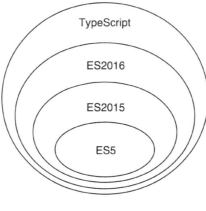

Figure 1

As TypeScript is statically typed, it can provide a number of benefits to us as JavaScript developers. Let's take a quick look at those benefits now.

Compile-time type checking

One of the most common mistakes we make while writing JavaScript code is to misspell a property or a method name. Usually, we find out about the mistake when we get a runtime error. This can happen during development as well as during production. Hoping that we will know about the error before we deploy our code to the production environment isn't a comfortable feeling! However, this is not a problem specific to JavaScript; it is something common to all the dynamic languages. Even with lots of unit tests, these errors can slip by.

TypeScript provides a compiler, which takes care of such mistakes for us by using static code analysis. If we take advantage of static typing, TypeScript will be aware of the existing properties a given object has, and if we misspell any of them, the compiler will warn us with a compile-time error.

Another great benefit of TypeScript is that it allows large teams to collaborate since it provides formal, verifiable naming. This way, it allows us to write easy-to-understand code.

Better support by text editors and IDEs

There are a number of tools, such as Tern, that are trying to bring better autocompletion support for JavaScript in text editors and IDEs. However, as JavaScript is a dynamic language, it is impossible for the IDEs and text editors to make sophisticated suggestions without any metadata. Google Closure Compiler, for instance, uses type annotations provided in the JSDoc in order to provide static typing to the language.

Annotating the code with such metadata is a built-in feature of TypeScript known as type annotations. Based on them, text editors and IDEs can perform a better static analysis on our code. This provides better refactoring tools and autocompletion, which increases our productivity and allows us to make fewer mistakes while writing the source code for our applications.

There's even more to TypeScript

TypeScript by itself has a number of other benefits:

- **It is a superset of JavaScript**: All JavaScript programs (for example, ES5 and ES2015) are already valid TypeScript ones. In essence, you have already been writing TypeScript code. Since it is based on the latest version of the ECMAScript standard, it allows us to take advantage of the latest bleeding-edge syntax provided by the language.
- **Supports optional type checking**: If, for any reason, we decide that we don't want to explicitly define the type of a variable or a method, we can just skip the type definition. However, we should be aware that this means we are no longer taking advantage of the static typing, so we are giving up on all the benefits mentioned earlier.
- **Developed and maintained by Microsoft**: The quality of the implementation of the language is very high, and it is unlikely that support will be dropped unexpectedly. TypeScript is based on the work of some of the world's best experts in programming language development.
- **It is open source**: This allows the community to freely contribute to the language and suggest features, which are discussed in an open manner. The fact that TypeScript is open source makes the development of third-party extensions and tools easier. This extends the scope of its usage even further.

Since modern browsers do not support TypeScript natively, there is a compiler that translates the TypeScript code we write into readable JavaScript in a predefined target version of ECMAScript. Once the code is compiled, all the type annotations are removed.

Using TypeScript

Let's start writing some TypeScript!

In the following sections, we will take a look at different snippets showing some of the features of TypeScript. In order to be able to run the snippets and play with them yourself, you'll need to install the TypeScript compiler on your computer. Let's take a look at how to do this.

TypeScript is best installed using **Node Package Manager** (**npm**). I'd recommend that you use npm's version 3.0.0 or newer. If you don't have node.js and npm installed already, you can visit `https://nodejs.org`and follow the instructions there.

Installing TypeScript with npm

Once you have npm installed and running, verify that you have the latest version by opening your terminal window and running the following command:

```
$ npm -v
```

Use the following command in order to install TypeScript 2.1.0 or newer:

```
$ npm install -g typescript@^2.1.0
```

The preceding command will install the TypeScript compiler and add its executable (`tsc`) as global.

In order to verify that everything works properly, you can use the following command:

```
$ tsc -v
Version 2.1.1
```

The output should be similar to the preceding one, though possibly with a different version.

Note that we install TypeScript by prefixing the version with caret. This means that npm will download any version in the range 2.x.x, but below 3.0.0.

Running our first TypeScript program

Now, let's compile our first TypeScript program! Create a file called `hello.ts` and enter the following content:

```
// ch3/hello-world/hello-world.ts

console.log('Hello world!');
```

Since we've already installed the TypeScript compiler, you should have a global executable command called `tsc`. You can use it in order to compile the file:

```
$ tsc hello.ts
```

Now, you should see the file `hello.js` in the same directory where `hello.ts` is. `hello.js` is the output of the TypeScript compiler; it contains the JavaScript equivalent to the TypeScript you wrote. You can run this file using the following command:

```
$ node hello.js
```

Now, you'll see the string **Hello world!** printed on the screen. In order to combine the process of compiling and running the program, you can use the `ts-node` package:

```
$ npm install -g ts-node
```

Now you can run:

```
$ ts-node hello.ts
```

You should see the same result, but without the `ts-node` file stored on the disk.

You can find the code for this book at `https://github.com/mgechev/getting-started-with-angular`. Most code snippets have a comment as the first line, which shows where you can find the complete example in the directory structure of the samples repository. Note that the paths are relative to the `app` directory.

TypeScript syntax and features introduced by ES2015 and ES2016

As TypeScript is a superset of JavaScript, before we start learning about its syntax, it'll be easier to start by introducing some of the bigger changes in ES2015 and ES2016; to understand TypeScript, we first must understand ES2015 and ES2016. We will have a whistle-stop tour through these changes before diving into TypeScript properly later.

A detailed explanation of ES2015 and ES2016 is outside the scope of this book. In order to get familiar with all the new features and syntaxes, I strongly recommend that you take a look at *Exploring ES6: Upgrade to the next version of JavaScript* by *Dr. Axel Rauschmayer*.

The next couple of pages will introduce new standards and allow you to take advantage of most of the features you will need during the development of Angular applications.

ES2015 arrow functions

JavaScript has first-class functions, which means that they can be passed around like any other value:

```
// ch3/arrow-functions/simple-reduce.ts

var result = [1, 2, 3].reduce(function (total, current) {
  return total + current;
}, 0); // 6
```

This syntax is great; however, it is a bit too verbose. ES2015 introduced a new syntax to define anonymous functions called the arrow function syntax. Using it, we can create anonymous functions, as seen in the following examples:

```
// ch3/arrow-functions/arrow-functions.ts

// example 1
var result = [1, 2, 3]
  .reduce((total, current) => total + current, 0);

console.log(result); // 6

// example 2
var even = [3, 1, 56, 7].filter(el => !(el % 2));

console.log(even); // [56]
```

```
// example 3
var sorted = data.sort((a, b) => {
  var diff = a.price - b.price;
  if (diff !== 0) {
    return diff;
  }
  return a.total - b.total;
});
```

In the first example, we got the total sum of the elements in the array [1, 2, 3]. In the second example, we got all the even numbers inside the array [3, 1, 56, 7]. In the third example, we sorted an array by the properties' price and total in ascending order.

Arrow functions have a few more features that we need to look at. The most important feature is that they keep the context (this) from the surrounding code:

```
// ch3/arrow-functions/context-demo.ts

function MyComponent() {
  this.age = 42;
  setTimeout(() => {
    this.age += 1;
    console.log(this.age);
  }, 100);
}

new MyComponent(); // 43 in 100ms.
```

For example, when we invoke the MyComponent function with the operator new; this will point to the new object instantiated by the call. The arrow function will keep the context (this), in the callback of setTimeout, and print **43** on the screen.

This is extremely useful in Angular since the binding context for a given component is its instance (that is, its this instance). If we define MyComponent as an Angular component and we have a binding to the age property, the preceding code will be valid and all the bindings will work (note that we don't have the scope, neither do we have explicit calls to the $digest loop, although we have called setTimeout directly).

Using the ES2015 and ES2016 classes

When developers new to JavaScript hear that the language empowers the **object-oriented (OO)** paradigm, they're normally confused when they discover that there's no syntax for the definition of classes. This perception was born by the fact that some of the most popular programming languages, such as Java, C#, and C++, have the concept of classes used for the construction of objects. However, JavaScript implements the OO paradigm differently. JavaScript has a prototype-based, object-oriented programming model, where we can instantiate objects using the object literal syntax or functions (also known as the constructor functions), and we can take advantage of the inheritance using the so-called prototype chain.

Although this is a valid way to implement the OO paradigm, and the semantics are similar to the one in the classical object-oriented model, it is confusing for inexperienced JavaScript developers who are not sure how to process this properly. This is one of the reasons TC39 decided to provide an alternative syntax to use the object-oriented paradigm in the language. Behind the scenes, the new syntax has the same semantics as the one we're used to, like using the constructor functions and the prototype-based inheritance. However, it provides a more convenient syntax to empower the OO paradigm's features with less boilerplate.

ES2016 adds some extra syntax to the ES2015 classes, such as static and instance property declaration.

Here is an example that demonstrates the syntax used to define the classes in ES2016:

```
// ch3/es6-classes/sample-classes.ts

class Human {
  static totalPeople = 0;
  _name; // ES2016 property declaration syntax

  constructor(name) {
    this._name = name;
    Human.totalPeople += 1;
  }

  get name() {
    return this._name;
  }

  set name(val) {
    this._name = val;
  }

  talk() {
    return `Hi, I'm ${this.name}!`;
  }
}

class Developer extends Human {
  _languages; // ES2016 property declaration syntax
```

```
  constructor(name, languages) {
    super(name);
    this._languages = languages;
  }

  get languages() {
    return this._languages;
  }

  talk() {
    return `${super.talk()} And I know ${this.languages.join(',')}.`;
  }
}
```

In ES2015, the explicit declaration of the _name property is not required; however, since the TypeScript compiler should be aware during compile time of the existing properties of the instances of a given class, we would need to add the declaration of the property to the class declaration itself.

The preceding snippet is both a valid TypeScript and JavaScript code. In it, we defined a class called Human, which adds a single property to the objects instantiated by it. It does this by setting the property's value to the value of the parameter name passed to its constructor.

Now, open the ch3/es6-classes/sample-classes.ts file and play around with it! You can create different instances of the classes in the same way you create objects using constructor functions:

```
var human = new Human('foobar');
var dev = new Developer('bar', ['JavaScript']);
console.log(dev.talk());
```

In order to execute the code, run the following command:

```
$ ts-node sample-classes.ts
```

Classes are commonly used in Angular. You can use them to define your components, directives, services, and pipes. However, you can also use the alternative ES5 syntax, which takes advantage of the constructor functions. Under the hood, once the TypeScript code is compiled, there would be no such significant difference between both the syntaxes, because the ES2015 classes are being transpiled to constructor functions anyway.

Defining variables with block scope

Another confusing point of JavaScript for developers with a different background is the variable scope in the language. In Java and C++, for example, we're used to the block lexical scope. This means that a given variable defined inside a specific block will be visible only inside that block and all of the nested blocks inside of it.

However, in JavaScript, things are a little bit different. ECMAScript defines a functional lexical scope that has similar semantics to the block lexical scope, but it uses functions instead of blocks. Lets take a look at the following code snippet:

```
// ch3/let/var.ts

var fns = [];
for (var i = 0; i < 5; i += 1) {
  fns.push(function() {
    console.log(i);
  });
}
fns.forEach(fn => fn());
```

This has some weird implications. Once the code is executed, it will log five times the number 5.

ES2015 added a new syntax to define variables with block scope visibility. The syntax is similar to the current one, however, instead of `var`, it uses the keyword `let`:

```
// ch3/let/let.ts

var fns = [];
for (let i = 0; i < 5; i += 1) {
  fns.push(function() {
    console.log(i);
  });
}
fns.forEach(fn => fn());
```

Meta-programming with ES2016 decorators

JavaScript is a dynamic language that allows us to easily modify and/or alter the behavior to suit the programs we write. Decorators are a proposal to ES2016, which according to the design document `https://github.com/wycats/javascript-decorators`:

> *"...make it possible to annotate and modify classes and properties at design time."*

Their syntaxes are quite similar to the annotations in Java, and they are even closer to the decorators in Python. ES2016 decorators are used commonly in Angular to define components, directives, and pipes, and to take advantage of the dependency injection mechanism of the framework. Most use cases of decorators involve altering the behavior to a predefined logic or adding some metadata to different constructs.

ES2016 decorators allow us to do a lot of fancy things by changing the behavior of our programs. Typical use cases could be to annotate the given methods or properties as deprecated or read-only. A set of predefined decorators that can improve the readability of the code we produce can be found in a project by *Jay Phelps* called *core-decorators.js*. Another use case is taking advantage of the proxy-based, aspect-oriented programming using a declarative syntax. The library providing this functionality is *aspect.js*.

In general, ES2016 decorators are just another syntax sugar, which translates to JavaScript code we're already familiar with from the previous versions of the language. Let's take a look at a simple example from the proposal's draft:

```
// ch3/decorators/nonenumerable.ts

class Person {
  @nonenumerable
  get kidCount() {
    return 42;
  }
}

function nonenumerable(target, name, descriptor) {
  descriptor.enumerable = false;
  return descriptor;
}

var person = new Person();

for (let prop in person) {
  console.log(prop);
}
```

In this case, we have an ES2015 class called `Person` with a single getter called `kidCount`. Over the `kidCount` getter, we have applied the `@nonenumerable` decorator. The decorator is a function that accepts a target (the `Person` class), the name of the target property we intend to decorate (`kidCount`), and the descriptor of the target property. After we change the descriptor, we need to return it in order to apply the modification. Basically, the decorator's application could be translated into ECMAScript 5 in the following way:

```
descriptor = nonenumerable(Person.prototype, 'kidCount', descriptor) ||
```

```
descriptor;
Object.defineProperty(Person.prototype, 'kidCount', descriptor);
```

Using configurable decorators

Here is an example of using the decorators defined by Angular:

```
@Component({
  selector: 'app',
  providers: [NamesList],
  templateUrl: './app.html',
})
export class App {}
```

When decorators accept arguments (just like `Component` in the preceding example), they need to be defined as functions that accept arguments and return the actual decorator:

```
function Component(config) {
  // validate properties
  return (componentCtrl) => {
    // apply decorator
  };
}
```

In this example, we defined a function `Component` that accepts a single argument called `config` and returns a decorator.

Writing modular code with ES2015

Another problem that JavaScript professionals have experienced over the years is the lack of a module system in the language. Initially, the community developed different patterns, aiming to enforce the modularity and the encapsulation of the software we produce. Such patterns included the module pattern, which takes advantage of the functional lexical scope and closures. Another example is the namespace pattern, which represents the different namespaces as nested objects. AngularJS introduced its own module system that unfortunately doesn't provide features, such as lazy module loading. However, these patterns were more like workarounds rather than real solutions.

CommonJS (used in node.js) and **AMD** (**Asynchronous Module Definition**) were later invented. They are still widely used today and provide features such as handling of circular dependencies, asynchronous module loading (in AMD), and so on.

TC39 took the best of the existing module systems and introduced this concept on a language level. ES2015 provides two APIs to define and consume modules. They are as follows:

- Declarative API.
- Imperative API using a module loader.

Angular takes full advantage of the ES2015 module system, so let's dive into it! In this section, we will take a look at the syntax used for the declarative definition and consumption of modules. We will also take a peek at the module loader's API in order to see how we can programmatically load modules in an explicit asynchronous manner.

Using the ES2015 module syntax

Let's take a look at an example:

```
// ch3/modules/math.ts

export function square(x) {
  return Math.pow(x, 2);
};

export function log10(x) {
  return Math.log10(x);
};

export const PI = Math.PI;
```

In the preceding snippet, we defined a simple ES2015 module in the math.ts file. We can think of it as a sample math Angular utility module. Inside it, we define and export the square and log10 functions and the constant PI. The const keyword is another keyword brought by ES2015 that is used to define constants. As you can see, what we do is nothing more than prefixing the function's definitions with the keyword export. If we want to export the entire functionality in the end and skip the duplicate explicit usage of export, we can use the following approach:

```
// ch3/modules/math2.ts

function square(x) {
  return Math.pow(x, 2);
};

function log10(x) {
  return Math.log10(x);
```

```
};

const PI = Math.PI;

export { square, log10, PI };
```

The syntax on the last line is nothing more than an enhanced object literal syntax, introduced by ES2015. Now, let's take a look at how we can consume this module:

```
// ch3/modules/app.ts

import {square, log10} from './math';

console.log(square(2)); // 4
console.log(log10(10)); // 1
```

As an identifier of the module, we use its relative path to the current file. Using destructuring, we import the required functions — in this case, `square` and `log10`.

Taking advantage of the modules' implicit asynchronous behavior

It is important to note that the ES2015 module syntax has implicit asynchronous behavior.

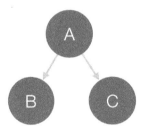

Figure 2

In the preceding diagram, we have modules A, B, and C. Module A uses modules B and C, so it depends on them. Once the user requires module A, the JavaScript module loader would need to load modules B and C before being able to invoke any of the logic that resides in module A because of the dependencies they have. Modules B and C will be loaded asynchronously. Once they are loaded completely, the JavaScript virtual machine will be able to execute module A.

Using aliases

Another typical situation is when we want to use an alias for a given export. For example, if we use a third-party library, we may want to rename any of its exports in order to escape name collisions or just to have a more convenient naming:

```
import {
  platformBrowserDynamic as platform
} from '@angular/platform-browser-dynamic';
```

Importing all the module exports

We can import the entire `math` module using the following syntax:

```
// ch3/modules/app2.ts

import * as math from './math';

console.log(math.square(2)); // 4
console.log(math.log10(10)); // 1
console.log(math.PI); // 3.141592653589793
```

The semantics behind this syntax is quite similar to CommonJS, although, in the browser, we have implicit asynchronous behavior.

Default exports

If a given module defines an export, which would quite likely be used by any of its consumer modules, we can take advantage of the default export syntax:

```
// ch3/modules/math3.ts

export default function cube(x) {
  return Math.pow(x, 3);
};

export function square(x) {
  return Math.pow(x, 2);
};
```

In order to consume this module, we can use the following `app.ts` file:

```
// ch3/modules/app3.ts
```

```
import cube from './math3';

console.log(cube(3)); // 27
```

Alternatively, if we want to import the default export and perform some other exports, we can use:

```
// ch3/modules/app4.ts

import cube, { square } from './math3';

console.log(square(2)); // 4
console.log(cube(3)); // 27
```

In general, the default export is nothing more than a named export named with the reserved word `default`:

```
// ch3/modules/app5.ts

import { default as cube } from './math3';

console.log(cube(3)); // 27
```

ES2015 module loader

The new version of the standard defines a programmatic API to work with modules. This is the so-called module loader API. It allows us to define and import modules, or configure the module loading.

Let's suppose we have the following module definition in the file `app.js`:

```
import { square } from './math';

export function main() {
  console.log(square(2)); // 4
}
```

From the `init.js` file, we can programmatically load the `app` module and invoke its `main` function using:

```
System.import('./app')
  .then(app => {
    app.main();
  })
```

```
    .catch(error => {
      console.log('Terrible error happened', error);
    });
```

The global object `System` has a method called `import` that allows us to import modules using their identifier. In the preceding snippet, we import the module `app` defined in `app.js`. `System.import` returns a promise that could be resolved on success or rejected in case of an error. Once the promise is resolved as the first parameter of the callback passed to `then`, we will get the module instance. The first parameter of the callback registered in case of rejection is an object representing the error that happened.

The code from the last snippet does not exist in the GitHub repository since it requires some additional configuration. We will apply the module loader more explicitly in the Angular examples in the later chapters of the book.

ES2015 and ES2016 recap

Congratulations! We're more than halfway toward learning TypeScript. All the features we just saw are a part of TypeScript since it implements a superset of JavaScript; since all these features are an upgrade on top of the current syntax, they are easy for experienced JavaScript developers to grasp.

In the next sections, we will describe all the amazing features of TypeScript that are outside the intersection with ECMAScript.

Taking advantage of static typing

Static typing is what can provide better tooling for our development process. While writing JavaScript, the most that IDEs and text editors can do is syntax highlight and provide some basic autocompletion suggestions based on sophisticated static analysis of our code. This means that we can only verify that we haven't made any typos by running the code.

In the previous sections, we described only the new features provided by ECMAScript expected to be implemented by browsers in the near future. In this section, we will take a look at what TypeScript provides in order to help us be less error-prone and more productive. At the time of writing this book, there were no plans to implement built-in support for static typing in the browsers.

The TypeScript code goes through intermediate preprocessing that performs the type checking and drops all the type annotations in order to provide valid JavaScript supported by modern browsers.

Using explicit type definitions

Just like Java and C++, TypeScript allows us to explicitly declare the type of the given variable:

```
let foo: number = 42;
```

The preceding line defines the variable `foo` in the current block using the `let` syntax. We explicitly declare that we want `foo` to be of the type `number` and we set the value of `foo` to `42`.

Now, let's try to change the value of `foo`:

```
let foo: number = 42;
foo = '42';
```

Here, after the declaration of `foo`, we will set its value to the string `'42'`. This is a perfectly valid JavaScript code; however, if we compile it using the TypeScript's compiler, we will get:

```
$ tsc basic.ts
basic.ts(2,1): error TS2322: Type 'string' is not assignable to type
'number'.
```

Once `foo` is associated with the given type, we cannot assign it values belonging to different types. This is one of the reasons we can skip the explicit type definition in case we assign a value to the given variable:

```
let foo = 42;
foo = '42';
```

The semantics of this code will be the same as the one with the explicit type definition because of the type inference of TypeScript. We'll further take a look at it at the end of this chapter.

The type any

All the types in TypeScript are subtypes of a type called `any`. We can declare variables belonging to the `any` type using the `any` keyword. Such variables can hold the value of any type:

```
let foo: any;
foo = {};
foo = 'bar ';
foo += 42;
console.log(foo); // "bar 42"
```

The preceding code is a valid TypeScript, and it will not throw any error during compilation or runtime. If we use the type `any` for all of our variables, we will be basically writing the code with dynamic typing, which drops all the benefits of the TypeScript's compiler. That's why we have to be careful with `any` and use it only when it is necessary.

All the other types in TypeScript belong to one of the following categories:

- **Primitive types**: These include Number, String, Boolean, Void, Null, Undefined, and Enum types.
- **Union types**: These types are out of the scope of this book. You can take a look at them in the specification of TypeScript.
- **Object types**: These include Function types, classes and interface type references, array types, tuple types, function types, and constructor types.
- **Type parameters**: These include Generics that will be described in the *Writing generic code by using type parameters* section.

Understanding the Primitive types

Most of the primitive types in TypeScript are the ones we are already familiar with in JavaScript: Number, String, Boolean, Null, and Undefined. So, we will skip their formal explanation here. Another set of types that is handy while developing Angular applications is the Enum types defined by users.

The Enum types

The Enum types are primitive user-defined types that, according to the specification, are subclasses of Number. The concept of enums exists in the Java, C++, and C# languages, and it has the same semantics in TypeScript–user-defined types consisting of sets of named values called elements. In TypeScript, we can define an enum using the following syntax:

```
enum STATES {
  CONNECTING,
  CONNECTED,
  DISCONNECTING,
  WAITING,
  DISCONNECTED
};
```

This will be translated to the following JavaScript:

```
var STATES;
(function (STATES) {
    STATES[STATES["CONNECTING"] = 0] = "CONNECTING";
    STATES[STATES["CONNECTED"] = 1] = "CONNECTED";
    STATES[STATES["DISCONNECTING"] = 2] = "DISCONNECTING";
    STATES[STATES["WAITING"] = 3] = "WAITING";
    STATES[STATES["DISCONNECTED"] = 4] = "DISCONNECTED";
})(STATES || (STATES = {}));
```

We can use the enum type as follows:

```
if (this.state === STATES.CONNECTING) {
  console.log('The system is connecting');
}
```

Understanding the Object types

In this section, we will take a look at the Array types and Function types, which belong to the more generic class of Object types. We will also explore how we can define classes and interfaces. Tuple types were introduced by TypeScript 1.3, and their main purpose is to allow the language to begin typing the new features introduced by ES2015, such as destructuring. We will not describe them in this book. For further reading, you can take a look at the language's specification at `http://www.typescriptlang.org`.

The Array types

In TypeScript, arrays are JavaScript arrays with a common element type. This means that we cannot have elements from different types in a given array. We have different array types for all the built-in types in TypeScript, plus all the custom types that we define.

We can define an array of numbers as follows:

```
let primes: number[] = [];
primes.push(2);
primes.push(3);
```

If we want to have an array, which seems heterogeneous, similar to the arrays in JavaScript, we can use the type reference to `any`:

```
let randomItems: any[] = [];
randomItems.push(1);
randomItems.push('foo');
randomItems.push([]);
randomItems.push({});
```

This is possible since the types of all the values we're pushing to the array are subtypes of the `any` type and the array we've declared contains values of the type `any`.

We can use the array methods we're familiar with in JavaScript with all the TypeScript Array types:

```
let randomItems: any[] = [];
randomItems.push('foo');
randomItems.push('bar');
randomItems.join(''); // foobar
randomItems.splice(1, 0, 'baz');
randomItems.join(''); // foobazbar
```

We also have the square-brackets operator that gives us random access to the array's elements:

```
let randomItems: any[] = [];
randomItems.push('foo');
randomItems.push('bar');
randomItems[0] === 'foo'
randomItems[1] === 'bar'
```

The Function types

We're already familiar with how to define a new function in JavaScript. We can use function expression or function declaration:

```
// function expression
var isPrime = function (n) {
  // body
};

// function declaration
function isPrime(n) {
  // body
};
```

Alternatively, we can use the new arrow function syntax:

```
var isPrime = n => {
  // body
};
```

The only thing TypeScript alters is the feature to define the types of the function's arguments and the type of its return result (i.e. the function's signature). After the compiler of the language performs its type checking and transpilation, all the type annotations will be removed. If we use function expression and assign a function to a variable, we will be able to define the variable type in the following way:

```
let variable: (arg1: type1, arg2: type2, ..., argn: typen) => returnType
```

Consider the following example:

```
let isPrime: (n: number) => boolean = n => {
  // body
};
```

If we want to define a method in an object literal, we can do it in the following way:

```
let math = {
  squareRoot(n: number): number {
    // ...
  }
};
```

In the preceding example, we defined an object literal with method called `squareRoot` using the ES2015 syntax.

In case we want to define a function that produces some side effects instead of returning a result, we can declare it's return type as `void`:

```
let person = {
  _name: null,
  setName(name: string): void {
    this._name = name;
  }
};
```

Defining classes

TypeScript classes are similar to what ES2015 offers. However, it alters the type declarations and adds more syntax sugar. For example, let's take the `Human` class we defined earlier and make it a valid TypeScript class:

```
class Human {
  static totalPeople = 0;
  _name: string;

  constructor(name) {
    this._name = name;
    Human.totalPeople += 1;
  }

  get name() {
    return this._name;
  }

  set name(val) {
    this._name = val;
  }

  talk() {
    return `Hi, I'm ${this.name}!`;
  }
}
```

There is no difference between the current TypeScript definition with the one we already introduced; however, in this case, the declaration of the _name property is mandatory. Here is how we can use the class:

```
let human = new Human('foo');
console.log(human._name);
```

Using access modifiers

Similarly, for most conventional object-oriented languages that support classes, TypeScript allows a definition of access modifiers. In order to deny direct access to the _name property outside the class it is defined in, we can declare it as private:

```
class Human {
  static totalPeople = 0;
  private _name: string;
  // ...
}
```

The supported access modifiers by TypeScript are as follows:

- **Public**: All the properties and methods declared as public can be accessed from anywhere.
- **Private**: All the properties and methods declared as private can be accessed only from inside the class' definition itself.
- **Protected**: All the properties and methods declared as protected can be accessed from inside the class' definition or the definition of any other class extending the one that owns the property or the method.

Access modifiers are a great way to implement Angular services with good encapsulation and a well-defined interface. In order to understand it better, let's take a look at an example using the class' hierarchy defined earlier, which is ported to TypeScript:

```
class Human {
  static totalPeople = 0;

  constructor(protected name: string, private age: number) {
    Human.totalPeople += 1;
  }

  talk() {
    return `Hi, I'm ${this.name}!`;
  }
}

class Developer extends Human {
  constructor(name: string, private languages: string[], age: number) {
    super(name, age);
  }

  talk() {
    return `${super.talk()} And I know ${this.languages.join(', ')}.`;
  }
```

```
}
```

Just like ES2015, TypeScript supports the `extends` keyword and desugars it to the prototypal JavaScript inheritance.

In the preceding example, we set the access modifiers of the `name` and `age` properties directly inside the constructor function. The semantics behind this syntax differs from the one used in the previous example. It has the following meaning: define a protected property called `name` of the type `string` and assign the first value passed to the constructor call to it. It is the same for the private `age` property. This saves us from explicitly setting the value in the constructor itself. If we take a look at the constructor of the `Developer` class, we can see that we can use the mixture between these syntaxes. We can explicitly define the property in the constructor's signature, or we can only define that the constructor accepts a parameters of the given types.

Now, let's create a new instance of the `Developer` class:

```
let dev = new Developer('foo', ['JavaScript', 'Go'], 42);
dev.languages = ['Java'];
```

During compilation, TypeScript will throw an error telling us that: **Property languages is private and only accessible inside the class "Developer"**. Now, let's see what will happen if we create a new `Human` class and try to access its properties from outside its definition:

```
let human = new Human('foo', 42);
human.age = 42;
human.name = 'bar';
```

In this case, we'll get the following two errors:

Property age is private and is only accessible inside the class "Human", and the **Property name is a protected and only accessible inside class "Human" and its subclasses**.

However, if we try to access the _name property from inside the definition of `Developer`, the compiler won't throw any errors.

In order to get a better sense of what the TypeScript compiler will produce out of a type-annotated class, let's take a look at the JavaScript produced by the following definition:

```
class Human {
  constructor(private name: string) {}
}
```

The resulting ECMAScript 5 will be as follows:

```
var Human = (function () {
    function Human(name) {
        this.name = name;
    }
    return Human;
})();
```

The defined property is added directly to the objects instantiated by calling the constructor function with the operator `new`. This means that once the code is compiled, we can directly access the private members of the created objects. In order to wrap this up, access modifiers are added in the language in order to help us enforce better encapsulation and get compile-time errors in case we violate it.

Defining interfaces

Subtyping in programming languages allows us to treat objects in the same way based on the observation that they are specialized versions of a generic object. This doesn't mean that they have to be instances of the same class of objects, or that they have a complete intersection between their interfaces. The objects might have only a few common properties and still be treated the same way in a specific context. In JavaScript, we usually use duck typing. We may invoke specific methods for all the objects passed to a function based on the assumption that these methods exist. However, all of us have experienced the **undefined is not a function** error thrown by the JavaScript interpreter.

Object-oriented programming and TypeScript come with a solution. They allow us to make sure that our objects have similar behavior if they implement interfaces that declare the subset of the properties they own.

For example, we can define our interface `Accountable`:

```
interface Accountable {
  getIncome(): number;
}
```

Now, we can make sure that both `Individual` and `Firm` implement this interface by performing the following:

```
class Firm implements Accountable {
  getIncome(): number {
    // ...
  }
}
```

```
class Individual implements Accountable {
  getIncome(): number {
    // ...
  }
}
```

In case we implement a given interface, we need to provide an implementation for all the methods defined inside it, otherwise, the TypeScript compiler will throw an error. The methods we implement must have the same signature as the ones declared in the interface definition.

TypeScript interfaces also support properties. In the `Accountable` interface, we can include a field called `accountNumber` with a type of string:

```
interface Accountable {
  accountNumber: string;
  getIncome(): number;
}
```

We can define it in our class as a field or a getter.

Interface inheritance

Interfaces may also extend each other. For example, we may turn our `Individual` class into an interface that has a social security number:

```
interface Accountable {
  accountNumber: string;
  getIncome(): number;
}

interface Individual extends Accountable {
  ssn: string;
}
```

Since interfaces support multiple inheritances, `Individual` may also extend the interface `Human` that has the `name` and `age` properties:

```
interface Accountable {
  accountNumber: string;
  getIncome(): number;
}

interface Human {
  age: number;
  name: number;
```

```
}

interface Individual extends Accountable, Human {
  ssn: string;
}
```

Implementing multiple interfaces

In case the class's behavior is a union of the properties defined in a couple of interfaces, it may implement all of them:

```
class Person implements Human, Accountable {
  age: number;
  name: string;
  accountNumber: string;

  getIncome(): number {
    // ...
  }
}
```

In this case, we need to provide the implementation of all the methods declared inside the interfaces our class implements, otherwise, the compiler will throw a compile-time error.

Further expressiveness with TypeScript decorators

In ES2015, we are able to decorate only classes, properties, methods, getters, and setters. TypeScript takes this further by allowing us to decorate functions or method parameters:

```
class Http {
  // ...
}

class GitHubApi {
  constructor(@Inject(Http) http) {
    // ...
  }
}
```

Keep in mind that the parameter decorators should not alter any additional behavior. Instead, they are used to generate metadata. The most typical use case of these decorators is the dependency injection mechanism of Angular.

Writing generic code by using type parameters

In the beginning of the section on using static typing, we mentioned the type parameters. In order to get a better understanding of them, let's begin with an example. Let's suppose that we want to implement the classical data structure `BinarySearchTree`. Let's define its interface using a class without applying any method implementations:

```
class Node {
  value: any;
  left: Node;
  right: Node;
}

class BinarySearchTree {
  private root: Node;
  insert(any: value): void { /* ... */ }
  remove(any: value): void { /* ... */ }
  exists(any: value): boolean { /* ... */ }
  inorder(callback: {(value: any): void}): void { /* ... */ }
}
```

In the preceding snippet, we defined a class called `Node`. The instances of this class represent the individual nodes in our tree. Each `node` has a left and a right child node and a value of the type `any`; we use `any` in order to be able to store data of any type inside our nodes and respectively inside `BinarySearchTree`.

Although the earlier implementation looks reasonable, we're giving up on using the most important feature that TypeScript provides, that is, static typing. Using `any` as a type of the value field inside the `Node` class, we can't take complete advantage of the compile-time type checking. This also limits the features that IDEs and text editors provide when we access the `value` property of the instances of the `Node` class.

TypeScript comes with an elegant solution that is already widely popular in the world of static typing–type parameters. Using generics, we can parameterize the classes we create with the type parameters. For example, we can turn our `Node` class into the following:

```
class Node<T> {
  value: T;
  left: Node<T>;
  right: Node<T>;
}
```

Node<T> indicates that this class has a single type parameter called T that is used somewhere inside the class's definition. We can use Node by performing the following snippet:

```
let numberNode = new Node<number>();
let stringNode = new Node<string>();
numberNode.right = new Node<number>();
numberNode.value = 42;
numberNode.value = '42'; // Type "string" is not assignable to type
"number"
numberNode.left = stringNode; // Type Node<string> is not assignable to
type Node<number>
```

In the preceding snippet, we created three nodes: numberNode, stringNode, and another node of the type Node<number>, assigning its value to the right child of numberNode. Note that since numberNode is of the type Node<number>, we can set its value to 42, but we can't use the string '42'. The same is applicable to its left child. In the definition, we've explicitly declared that we want the left and right children to be of the type Node<number>. This means that we cannot assign values of the type Node<string> to them; that's why, we get the second compile-time error.

Using generic functions

Another typical use of generics is for defining functions that operate over a set of types. For example, we may define an identity function that accepts an argument of type T and returns it:

```
function identity<T>(arg: T) {
  return arg;
}
```

However, in some cases, we may want to use only the instances of the types that have some specific properties. For achieving this, we can use an extended syntax that allows us to declare that we want the types used as type parameters to be subtypes of given type:

```
interface Comparable {
  compare(a: Comparable): number;
}

function sort<T extends Comparable>(arr: Comparable[]): Comparable[] {
  // ...
}
```

For example, here, we defined an interface called `Comparable`. It has a single operation called `compare`. The classes that implement the `Comparable` interface need to implement the `compare` operation. When `compare` is called with a given argument, it returns 1 if the target object is bigger than the passed argument, 0 if they are equal, and -1 if the target object is smaller than the passed argument.

Having multiple type parameters

TypeScript allows us to use multiple type parameters:

```
class Pair<K, V> {
  key: K;
  value: V;
}
```

In this case, we can create an instance of the class `Pair<K, V>` using the following syntax:

```
let pair = new Pair<string, number>();
pair.key = 'foo';
pair.value = 42;
```

Writing less verbose code with TypeScript's type inference

Static typing has a number of benefits; however, it makes us write a more verbose code by adding all the type annotations.

In some cases, the TypeScript's compiler is able to guess the types of expressions inside our code; let's consider this example, for instance:

```
let answer = 42;
answer = '42'; // Type "string" is not assignable to type "number"
```

In the preceding example, we defined a variable `answer` and assigned the value 42 to it. Since TypeScript is statically typed and the type of a variable cannot change once declared, the compiler is smart enough to guess that the type of `answer` is `number`.

If we don't assign a value to a variable within its definition, the compiler will set its type to any:

```
let answer;
answer = 42;
answer = '42';
```

The preceding snippet will compile without any compile-time errors.

Best common type

Sometimes, the type inference could be a result of several expressions. Such is the case when we assign a heterogeneous array to a variable:

```
let x = ['42', 42];
```

In this case, the type of x will be any[]. However, suppose we have the following:

```
let x = [42, null, 32];
```

The type of x will then be number[] since the type Number is a subtype of Null.

Contextual type inference

Contextual typing occurs when the type of an expression is implied from its location; let's take this example:

```
document.body.addEventListener('mousedown', e => {
  e.foo(); // Property "foo" does not exists on a type "MouseEvent"
}, false);
```

In this case, the type of the argument of the callback e is *guessed* by the compiler based on the context in which it is used. The compiler understands that the type of e is based on the call of addEventListener and the arguments passed to the method. In case we were using a keyboard event (keydown, for example), TypeScript would have been aware that e is of the type KeyboardEvent.

Type inference is a mechanism that allows us to write less verbose code by taking advantage of the static analysis performed by TypeScript. Based on the context, TypeScript's compiler is able to guess the type of a given expression without explicit definition.

Using ambient type definitions

Although static typing is amazing, most of the frontend libraries we use are built with JavaScript, which is dynamically typed. Since we'd want to use TypeScript in Angular, not having type definitions in the code that uses external JavaScript libraries is a big issue; it prevents us from taking advantage of the compile-time type checking.

TypeScript was built keeping these points in mind. In order to allow the TypeScript compiler to take care of what it does best, we can use the so-called ambient type definitions. They allow us to provide external type definitions of the existing JavaScript libraries. This way, they provide hints to the compiler.

Using predefined ambient type definitions

Fortunately, we don't have to create ambient type definitions for all JavaScript libraries and frameworks we use. The community and/or the authors of these libraries have already published such definitions online; the biggest repository resides at `https://github.com/DefinitelyTyped/DefinitelyTyped`. During the last couple of months, the community developed a few tools for managing ambient type definitions, such as `tsd` and `typings`.

Later, Microsoft introduced an official way to manage them, using `npm` by providing an additional configuration in `tsconfig.json`. The type definitions are now distributed as scoped packages under the namespace `@types` and installed in `node_modules`.

Let's create a directory and add a `package.json` file to it:

```
$ mkdir types-test && cd types-test && npm init
```

After we provide the default values for the questions that `npm` asks us, our `package.json` in the `types-test` directory should look something like this:

```
{
  "name": "types-test",
  "version": "1.0.0",
  "description": "",
  "main": "index.js",
  "scripts": {
    "test": "echo "Error: no test specified" && exit 1"
  },
  "author": "",
  "license": "ISC"
}
```

We can install new type definition using:

```
$ npm install @types/angular --save-dev
```

The preceding command will download the type definitions for AngularJS and save them in node_modules/@types/angular. Note that we provided the --save-dev flag to npm in order to save the type definition under devDependencies of package.json.

 When installing ambient type definitions we would usually use --save-dev instead of --save, because the definitions are mostly used in development.

After running the preceding command, your package.json file should look similar to this:

```
{
  "name": "types-test",
  "version": "1.0.0",
  "description": "",
  "main": "index.js",
  "scripts": {
    "test": "echo "Error: no test specified" && exit 1"
  },
  "author": "",
  "license": "ISC",
  "devDependencies": {
    "@types/angular": "^1.5.20"
  }
}
```

Now, in order to use AngularJS with TypeScript, create app.ts and enter the following content:

```
/// <reference path="./node_modules/@types/angular/index.d.ts"/>

var module = angular.module('module', []);
module.controller('MainCtrl',
  function MainCtrl($scope: angular.IScope) {

  });
```

To compile app.ts, use:

```
$ tsc app.ts
```

The TypeScript compiler will output the compiled content into `app.js`. In order to add extra automation and invoke the TypeScript compiler each time you change any of the files in your project, you can use a task runner, such as gulp or grunt, or pass the `-w` option to `tsc`.

 Since using the `reference` element for including type definitions is considered bad practice, we can use a `tsconfig.json` file instead. There, we can configure which directories need to be included in the compilation process by `tsc`. For more information, visit `http://www.typescriptlang.org/docs/handbook/tsconfig-json.html`.

Now, let's create a file called `tsconfig.json` in the same directory, with the following content:

```
{
  "compilerOptions": {
    "target": "es5",
    "module": "commonjs",
    "experimentalDecorators": true,
    "outDir": "./dist"
  },
  "files": [
    "./app.ts"
  ]
}
```

In this configuration file, we provide the `compilerOptions` property so that we don't have to pass parameters, such as `outDir` and `module` formats, as flags to `tsc`. Note that in the `files` property, we also list the files that we want to be compiled. TypeScript will compile all of them plus all their transitive dependencies!

Now, let's modify our preceding simple snippet:

```
var module = angular.module('module', []);
module.controller('MainCtrl',
  function MainCtrl($scope: angular.IScope) {
    const set = new Set<any>();
});
```

The only change we made was to add the line where we declare and initialize a new constant with the returned result by the invocation of the `Set` constructor function, with `any` as the type parameter. By having `tsconfig.json` in the same directory where our `app.ts` file and `node_modules` are, we can compile the project by running:

```
$ tsc
```

However, we'll get the following error:

demo.ts(4,22): error TS2304: Cannot find name 'Set'.

Set implements the set data structure and is part of the ES2015 standard. Since using the ambient type definitions for ES2015 is a very common practice in all TypeScript projects, Microsoft added them as part of TypeScript itself. To the compilerOptions property inside tsconfig.json, add the following lib property:

```
{
  "compilerOptions": {
    "target": "es5",
    "module": "commonjs",
    "experimentalDecorators": true,
    "outDir": "./dist",
    "lib": ["es2015", "dom"]
  },
  "files": [
    "./demo.ts"
  ]
}
```

lib has value an array, which includes both "es2015" and "dom" because we need ES2015 Set, and Angular's type definitions require the type definitions for the **Document Object Model (DOM)**. Now when you run tsc in the directory where your tsconfig.json file is located, the compilation process should pass successfully and the output file should be located in ./dist/demo.js.

Custom ambient type definitions

To understand how everything works together, let's take a look at an example. Suppose we have the following interface of a JavaScript library:

```
var DOM = {
  // Returns a set of elements which match the passed selector
  selectElements: function (selector) {
    // ...
  },
  hide: function (element) {
    // ...
  },
  show: function (element) {
    // ...
  }
};
```

We have an object literal assigned to a variable called DOM. The object has the following methods:

- selectElements: This accepts a single argument with type string and returns a set of DOM elements.
- hide: This accepts a DOM node as an argument and returns nothing.
- show: This accepts a DOM node as an argument and returns nothing.

In TypeScript, the preceding definition would look as follows:

```
var DOM = {
  // Returns a set of elements which match the passed selector
  selectElements: function (selector: string): HTMLElement[] {
    //...
    return [];
  },
  hide: function (element: HTMLElement): void {
    element.hidden = true;
  },
  show: function (element: HTMLElement): void {
    element.hidden = false;
  }
};
```

This means that we can define our library's interface as follows:

```
interface LibraryInterface {
  selectElements(selector: string): HTMLElement[]
  hide(element: HTMLElement): void
  show(element: HTMLElement): void
}
```

After we have the interface of our library, it will be easy to create the ambient type definition; we just have to create a file with an extension d.ts called dom and enter the following content:

```
// inside "dom.d.ts"

interface DOMLibraryInterface {
  selectElements(selector: string): HTMLElement[]
  hide(element: HTMLElement): void
  show(element: HTMLElement): void
}

declare var DOM: DOMLibraryInterface;
```

In the preceding snippet, we defined the interface called `DOMLibraryInterface` and declared the `DOM` variable of the type `DOMLibraryInterface`.

The only thing left before being able to use static typing with our JavaScript library is including the external type definition in the script files we want to use our library in. We can do it as follows:

```
/// <reference path="dom.d.ts"/>
```

The preceding snippet hints the compiler on where to find the ambient type definitions. An alternative, and better, way to provide a reference to the `d.ts` file is to use `tsconfig.json` as described above.

Summary

In this chapter, we peeked at the TypeScript language that is used for the implementation of Angular. Although we can develop our Angular applications using ECMAScript 5, Google's recommendation is to use TypeScript in order to take advantage of the static typing it provides.

While exploring the language, we looked at some of the core features of ES2015 and ES2016. We explained the ES2015 and ES2016 classes, arrow functions, block scope variable definitions, destructuring, and modules. Since Angular takes advantage of the ES2016 decorators, and more accurately their extension in TypeScript, a section was dedicated to them.

After this, we took a look at how we can take advantage of static typing using explicit type definitions. We described some of the built-in types in TypeScript and how we can define classes in the language by specifying access modifiers for their members. Our next stop was the interfaces. We ended our adventures in TypeScript by explaining the type parameters and the ambient type definitions.

In the next chapter, we will start exploring Angular in depth using the framework's components and directives.

4
Getting Started with Angular Components and Directives

By this point, we're already familiar with the core building blocks that Angular provides for the development of single-page applications and the relations between them. However, we've touched only the surface by introducing the general idea behind Angular's concepts and the basic syntax used for their definition. In this chapter, we'll take a deep dive into Angular's components and directives.

In the following sections, we will cover these topics:

- Enforced separation of concerns of the building blocks that Angular provides for developing applications.
- The appropriate use of directives or components when interacting with the DOM.
- Built-in directives and developing custom ones.
- An in-depth look at components and their templates.
- Content projection.
- View children versus content children.
- The component's life cycle.
- Using template references.
- Configuring Angular's change detection.

The "Hello world!" application in Angular

Now, let's build our first "Hello world!" application in Angular. In order to get everything up and running as easy and quickly as possible, for our first application, we will use the ECMAScript 5 syntax with the transpiled bundle of Angular. First, create the `index.html` file with the following content:

```html
<!-- ch4/es5/hello-world/index.html -->

<!DOCTYPE html>
<html lang="en">
<head>
  <meta charset="UTF-8">
  <title></title>
</head>
<body>
  <script src="https://unpkg.com/zone.js@0.6.25/dist/zone.js"></script>
  <script
src="https://unpkg.com/reflect-metadata@0.1.3/Reflect.js"></script>
  <script src="https://unpkg.com/rxjs@5.0.1/bundles/Rx.js"></script>
  <script
src="https://unpkg.com/@angular/core@2.2.0/bundles/core.umd.js"></script>
  <script
src="https://unpkg.com/@angular/common@2.2.0/bundles/common.umd.js"></scrip
t>
  <script
src="https://unpkg.com/@angular/compiler@2.2.0/bundles/compiler.umd.js"></s
cript>
  <script
src="https://unpkg.com/@angular/platform-browser@2.2.0/bundles/platform-bro
wser.umd.js"></script>
  <script
src="https://unpkg.com/@angular/platform-browser-dynamic@2.2.0/bundles/plat
form-browser-dynamic.umd.js"></script>
  <script src="./app.js"></script>
</body>
</html>
```

 Note that the examples in this book are built with Angular 2.2.0. In case you're using a newer version of the framework there might be slight differences. For further information take a look at the changelog at `https://github.com/angular/angular/blob/master/CHANGELOG.md`.

The preceding HTML file defines the basic structure of our page. Just before closing the body tag, we have references to a few script files: polyfills (zone.js and reflect-metadata) required by the framework, RxJS, the ES5 bundles of different packages of Angular, and the file that contains the application we're going to build.

 RxJS is used by Angular's core in order to allow us to empower the reactive programming paradigm in our applications. In the following content, we will take only a shallow look at how we can take advantage of observables. For further information, you can visit the RxJS GitHub repository at https://github.com/ReactiveX/rxjs.

In the same directory where your index.html resides, create a file called app.js and enter the following content inside it:

```
// ch4/es5/hello-world/app.js

var App = ng.core.Component({
  selector: 'my-app',
  template: '<h1>Hello {{target}}!</h1>'
})
.Class({
  constructor: function () {
    this.target = 'world';
  }
});

var AppModule = ng.core.NgModule({
  imports: [ng.platformBrowser.BrowserModule],
  declarations: [App],
  bootstrap: [App]
})
.Class({
  constructor: function () {}
});

ng.platformBrowserDynamic
  .platformBrowserDynamic()
  .bootstrapModule(AppModule);
```

In the preceding snippet, we defined a component called App with an my-app selector. The component has the following template:

```
'<h1>Hello {{target}}!</h1>'
```

This syntax should already be familiar to you from AngularJS. When compiled in the context of the given component, the preceding snippet will interpolate the template with the result of the expression inside the curly brackets. In our case, the expression is simply the `target` variable.

To `Class`, we pass an object literal, which has a single method called `constructor`. This **DSL (domain-specific language)** provides an alternative way to define classes in ECMAScript 5. In the body of the `constructor` function, we add a property called `target` with a value of the `"world"` string. Right after that, we define our `AppModule` class. Note that every component on our application must be associated with a module. Inside the module, as explained in `Chapter 2`, *The Building Blocks of an Angular Application*, we define the declarations, imports, and the bootstrap component.

At the last line of the snippet, we invoke the `bootstrapModule` method of the object returned by the invocation of `ng.platformBrowserDynamic()`. As argument of `bootstrapModule`, we pass the `AppModule` we just defined.

Note that `bootstrapModule` is under the `ng.platformBrowserDynamic` namespace. This is due to the fact that the framework is built with different platforms in mind, such as the browser, NativeScript, and so on. By placing the bootstrap methods used by the different platforms under a separate namespace, Angular can implement different logic to initialize the application.

Now, if you open `index.html` with your browser, you should see some errors, as shown in the following screenshot:

Figure 1

This happened because we missed something quite important. We didn't use the root component anywhere inside `index.html`. In order to finish the application, add the following HTML element after the open tag of the body element:

```
<my-app></my-app>
```

Now, you can refresh your browser to see the following result:

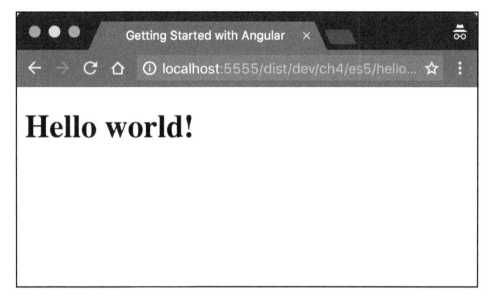

Figure 2

Using TypeScript

Although we already have an Angular application running, we can do much better! We didn't use any package manager or module loader. We spent all of `Chapter 3`, *TypeScript Crash Course*, talking about TypeScript; however, we didn't write a single line of it in the preceding application. Although it is not required that you use TypeScript with Angular, it's more convenient to take advantage of all the bonuses that static typing provides. By using TypeScript, we can also use the Ahead-of-Time compilation in Angular.

Setting up our environment

The core team of Angular developed a brand new CLI tool for Angular, which allows us to bootstrap our applications with a few commands. Although we will introduce it in the final chapter, by then, in order to boost our learning experience, we will use the code located at `https://github.com/mgechev/getting-started-with-angular`. This repository includes all the examples in this book, in one big application. It has all the required dependencies declared in `package.json`, the definition of basic gulp tasks, such as the development server, the transpilation of your TypeScript code to ECMAScript 5, live-reload, and so on.

 The project that contains all the examples for this book is based on angular-seed (`https://github.com/mgechev/angular-seed`), which allows us to quickly bootstrap an Angular application.

In order to set up the `getting-started-with-angular` project, you'll need Git, Node.js v6.x.x, and npm up and running on your computer. If you have a different version of the Node.js installed, I recommend that you take a look at nvm (the Node.js version manager, which is available at `https://github.com/creationix/nvm`) or n (`https://www.npmjs.com/package/n`). Using these tools, you'll be able to have multiple versions of Node.js on your machine and switch between them with a single command via the command line.

Installing the sample project repository

Let's start by setting up the `getting-started-with-angular` project. Open your terminal and enter the following commands:

```
# Will clone the repository and save it to directory called
# getting-started-with-angular
$ git clone https://github.com/mgechev/getting-started-with-angular.git
$ cd getting-started-with-angular
$ npm install
```

The first line will clone the `getting-started-with-angular` project into a directory called `getting-started-with-angular`; after that we enter that directory.

The last step before being able to run the seed project is to install all the required dependencies using npm. This step may take a while depending on your Internet connection, so be patient and do not interrupt it. If you encounter any problems, do not hesitate to raise the issues at `https://github.com/mgechev/getting-started-with-angular/issues`.

The last step left is to start the development server:

```
$ npm start
```

When the process of the transpilation is completed, your browser will automatically open with `http://localhost:5555/dist/dev`. You should now see a view similar to what is shown in the following screenshot:

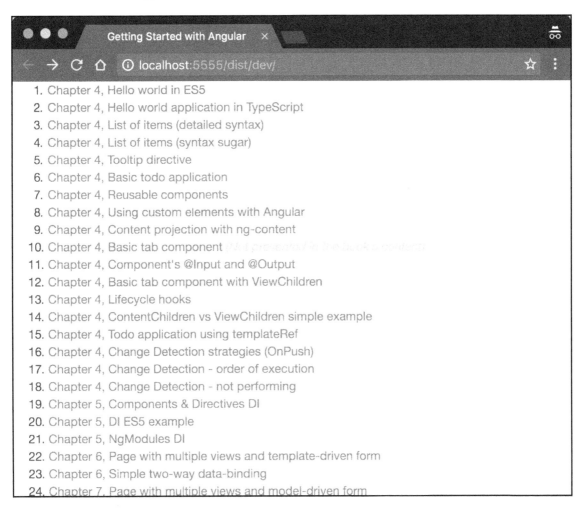

Figure 3

Playing with Angular and TypeScript

Now, let's play around with the files we already have. Navigate to the `app/ch4/ts/hello-world` directory inside `getting-started-with-angular`. Then, open `app.ts` and replace its content with the following snippet:

```
// ch4/ts/hello-world/app.ts

import {Component, NgModule} from '@angular/core';
import {BrowserModule} from '@angular/platform-browser';
import {platformBrowserDynamic} from '@angular/platform-browser-dynamic';

@Component({
  selector: 'my-app',
  templateUrl: './app.html'
})
class App {
  target: string;
  constructor() {
    this.target = 'world';
  }
}

@NgModule({
  declarations: [App],
  imports: [BrowserModule],
  bootstrap: [App],
})
class AppModule {}

platformBrowserDynamic().bootstrapModule(AppModule);
```

Let's take a look at the code line by line:

```
import {Component, NgModule} from '@angular/core';
import {BrowserModule} from '@angular/platform-browser';
import {platformBrowserDynamic} from '@angular/platform-browser-dynamic';
```

Initially, we import the `@Component` and `@NgModule` decorators from the `@angular/core` module, `BrowserModule` from `@angular/platform-browser` and the `platformBrowserDynamic` object from `@angular/platform-browser-dynamic`. Later, we use `@Component` to decorate the `App` class. To the `@Component` decorator, we pass the same object literal that we used in the ECMAScript 5 version of the application, but this time we reference to an external template.

As a next step, we define the view of the component. However, note that in this case, we use `templateUrl` instead of simply inlining the component's template.

Open `app.html` and replace the file's content with `<h1>Hello {{target}}!</h1>`. The content of `app.html` should be the same as the inlined template we have used previously. Since we can use a template by both inlining it (with `template`) and setting its URL (`templateUrl`), in some sense, the component's API is similar to the AngularJS directives API.

In the last line of the snippet, we bootstrap the application by providing the root module.

Now, let's take a look at `index.html` in order to get a sense of what goes on when we start the application:

```html
<!-- ch4/ts/hello-world/index.html -->
<!DOCTYPE html>
<html lang="en">
<head>
  <meta charset="utf-8">
  <meta http-equiv="X-UA-Compatible" content="IE=edge">
  <title><%= TITLE %></title>
  <meta name="description" content="">
  <meta name="viewport" content="width=device-width, initial-scale=1">
  <!-- inject:css -->
  <!-- endinject -->
</head>
<body>
  <my-app>Loading...</my-app>
  <!-- inject:js -->
  <!-- endinject -->
  <%= INIT %>
</body>
</html>
```

Note that inside the body of the page, we use the `my-app` element with content a text node with value `"Loading..."`. The `"Loading..."` label will be visible until the application gets bootstrapped and the main component gets rendered.

 There are template placeholders `<%= INIT %>` and `<-- inject:js...` that inject content that is specific to individual demos. They are not Angular specific, but instead aim to prevent code duplications in the code samples attached to the book because of the shared structure between them. In order to see how this specific HTML file has been transformed, open `/dist/dev/ch4/ts/hello-world/index.html`.

Using Angular directives

We have already built our simple "Hello world!" app. Now, let's start building something that is closer to a real-life application. By the end of this section, we'll have a simple application that lists a number of items we need to do and greets us at the header of the page.

Let's start by developing our `app` component. The two modifications from the preceding example that we need to make are renaming the `target` property to `name` and adding a list of `todos` to the component's controller definition:

```
// ch4/ts/ng-for/detailed-syntax/app.ts

import {Component, NgModule} from '@angular/core';
import {BrowserModule} from '@angular/platform-browser';
import {platformBrowserDynamic} from '@angular/platform-browser-dynamic';

@Component({
  selector: 'app',
  templateUrl: './app.html',
})
class App {
  todos: string[];
  name: string;
  constructor() {
    this.name = 'John';
    this.todos = ['Buy milk', 'Save the world'];
  }
}

@NgModule({
  declarations: [App],
  imports: [BrowserModule],
  bootstrap: [App],
})
class AppModule {}

platformBrowserDynamic().bootstrapModule(AppModule);
```

The only thing left is to update the template in order to consume the provided data. We're already familiar with the `ng-repeat` directive from AngularJS. It allows us to loop over a list of items using a microsyntax, which is later interpreted by AngularJS. However, the directive doesn't carry enough semantics, so it is hard to build tools that perform static code analysis and help us improve our development experience. Since the `ng-repeat` directive is quite useful, Angular kept the idea and improved it further in order to allow more sophisticated tooling by introducing further semantics on top of it. It allows IDEs and text editors to perform better static code analysis. Such support will prevent us from making typos in the code we write and allow us to have a smoother development experience.

In `app.html`, add the following content:

```
<!-- ch4/ts/ng-for/detailed-syntax/app.html -->

<h1>Hello {{name}}!</h1>
<p>
  Here's a list of the things you need to do:
</p>
<ul>
  <template ngFor let-todo [ngForOf]="todos">
    <li>{{todo}}</li>
  </template>
</ul>
```

 The `template` element is a place where we can hold markup and make sure that it won't be rendered by the browser. This is quite useful if we need to embed the templates of our application directly into the markup of the page and let the template engine we're using to process them at some point. In the current example, this means that if the Angular's DOM compiler doesn't process the DOM tree, we will not see the list item inside the `ul` element.

Now, after you refresh your browser, you should see the following result:

Figure 4

So far, so good! The only new things left in the preceding snippets are the attributes of the `template` element that we're not familiar with, such as `ngFor`, `let-todo`, and `[ngForOf]`. Let's take a look at them.

The ngFor directive

The `ngFor` directive is a directive that allows us to loop over a collection of items and does exactly what `ng-repeat` does in AngularJS, but it brings some extra semantics. Note that the `ngForOf` attribute is surrounded by brackets. At first, these brackets may seem like invalid HTML. However, according to the HTML specification, their use is permitted in attribute names. The only thing the W3C validator will complain about is the fact that the `template` element doesn't own such attributes; however, browsers won't have problems processing the markup.

The semantics behind these brackets is that the value of the attribute surrounded by them is an expression, which needs to be evaluated.

Improved semantics of the directives syntax

In `Chapter 1`, *Get Going with Angular*, we mentioned the opportunity for improved tooling in Angular. A big issue in AngularJS is the different ways in which we can use directives. This requires an understanding of the attribute values, which can be literals, expressions, callbacks, or a microsyntax. Starting with Angular 2, this problem is eliminated by introducing a few simple conventions that are built into the framework:

- `propertyName="value"`
- `[propertyName]="expression"`
- `(eventName)="handler()"`

In the first line, the `propertyName` attribute accepts a string literal as a value. Angular will not process the attribute's value any further; it will use it the way it is set in the template.

The second syntax, `[propertyName]="expression"`, gives a hint to Angular that the value of the attributes should be handled as an expression. When Angular finds an attribute surrounded by brackets, it will interpret the expression in the context of the component associated with the template. In short, if we want to set a nonstring value or the result of an expression as value of given property, we will need to use this syntax.

The last example shows how we can bind to events. The semantics behind `(eventName)="handler()"` is that we want to handle all events called `eventName` that are triggered by the given component with the `handler()` expression.

We will discuss more examples later in this chapter.

 Angular provides alternative canonical syntax, which allows us to define the bindings of the elements without using brackets. For instance, the property binding can be expressed using the following code:
`<input [value]="foo">`
It can also be expressed using this:
`<input bind-value="foo">`
Similarly, we can express the event bindings with the following code:
`<button (click)="handle()">Click me</button>`
They can also be expressed using this:
`<button on-click="handle()">Click me</button>`

Declaring variables inside a template

The last thing left from the preceding template is the `let-todo` attribute. Using this syntax, we are telling Angular that we want to declare a new variable called `todo` and bind it to the individual items from the collection we get from the evaluation of the expression set as a value of `[ngForOf]`.

Using syntax sugar in templates

Although the template syntax provides much more meaning of the code to the IDEs or text editors we use, it is quite verbose. Angular provides an alternative syntax, which will be desugared to the one shown in the preceding snippet.

There are a few Angular directives that require the usage of a template element, for example, `ngForOf`, `ngIf`, and `ngSwitch`. Since such directives are used often, there's an alternative syntax for them. Instead of typing down the entire template element explicitly, we can simply prefix the directive with `*`. This will allow us to turn our `ngForOf` directive syntax usage into the following:

```
<!-- ch4/ts/ng-for/syntax-sugar/app.html -->

<ul>
  <li *ngFor="let todo of todos">{{todo}}</li>
</ul>
```

Later, this template will be desugared by Angular to the more verbose syntax described earlier. Since the less verbose syntax is easier to read and write, its use is considered as the best practice.

 The `*` character allows us to remove the `template` element and put the directive directly on the top-level child element of the `template` (in the preceding example, the list item, `li`).

Defining Angular directives

Now that we've built a simple Angular component, let's continue our journey by understanding the Angular directives.

Using Angular directives, we can apply different behavioral or structural changes over the DOM. In this example, we will build a simple tooltip directive.

In contrast to components, directives do not have views and templates. Another core difference between these two concepts is that the given HTML element may have only a single component but multiple directives on it. In other words, directives augment the elements compared to components that are the actual elements in our views.

Angular's official style guide's recommendation is to use directives as attributes, prefixed with a namespace. Keeping this in mind, we will use the tooltip directive in the following way:

```
<div saTooltip="Hello world!"></div>
```

In the preceding snippet, we use the tooltip directive over the `div` element. As a namespace, its selector uses the `sa` string.

 Since the focus of the book is an efficient and intuitive learning of Angular's concepts, the code snippets may not completely align with the Angular style guide. However, for production applications, following best practices is essential. You can find the official Angular style guide at `https://angular.io/styleguide`.

Now, let's develop a tooltip directive! Before implementing it, we need to import a couple of symbols from `@angular/core`. Open a new TypeScript file called `app.ts` and enter the following content; we'll fill the placeholders later:

```
import {Directive, ElementRef, HostListener...} from '@angular/core';
```

In the preceding line, we import the following definitions:

- `ElementRef`: This allows us to inject the element reference (we're not limited to the DOM only) to the host element. In the sample usage of the preceding tooltip, we get an Angular wrapper of the `div` element, which holds the `saTooltip` attribute.
- `Directive`: This decorator allows us to add the metadata required for the new directives we define.
- `HostListener(eventname)`: This is a method decorator that accepts an event name as an argument. During initialization of the directive, Angular will add the decorated method as an event handler for the `eventname` events fired by the host element.

Let's look at the directive's implementation:

```
// ch4/ts/tooltip/app.ts

@Directive({
  selector: '[saTooltip]'
})
export class Tooltip {
  @Input() saTooltip:string;

  constructor(private el: ElementRef, private overlay: Overlay) {
    this.overlay.attach(el.nativeElement);
  }

  @HostListener('mouseenter')
  onMouseEnter() {
    this.overlay.open(this.el, this.saTooltip);
  }

  @HostListener('mouseleave')
  onMouseLeave() {
    this.overlay.close();
  }
}
```

Setting the directive's inputs

In the preceding example, we declared a directive with the `saTooltip` selector. Note that Angular's HTML compiler is case sensitive, which means that it will distinguish the `[satooltip]` and `[saTooltip]` selectors. After that, we declare the input of the directive using the @Input decorator over the saTooltip property. The semantics behind this code is that we declare a property called saTooltip and bind it to the value of the result that we got from the evaluation of the expression passed to the saTooltip attribute.

The @Input decorator accepts a single argument, that is, the name of the attribute we want to bind to. In case we don't pass an argument, Angular will create a binding between the attribute with the same name as the property itself. We will explain the concept of input and output in detail later in this chapter.

Understanding the directive's constructor

The constructor declares two private properties: el of the ElementRef type and overlay of the Overlay type. The Overlay class implements logic to manage the tooltips' overlays and will be injected using the DI mechanism of Angular. In order to declare it as available for injection, we will need to declare the top-level component in the following way:

```
@Component({
  selector: 'app',
  templateUrl: './app.html',
  providers: [Overlay],
  // ...
})
class App {}
```

 We will take a look at the dependency injection mechanism of Angular in the next chapter, where we will explain the way in which we can declare the dependencies of our services, directives, and components.
The implementation of the Overlay class is not important for the purpose of this chapter. However, if you're interested in it, you can find the implementation at ch4/ts/tooltip/app.ts.

Better encapsulation of directives with NgModules

In order to make the tooltip directive available to the Angular's compiler, we will need to explicitly declare where we intend to use it. For instance, take a look at the AppModule class at ch4/ts/tooltip/app.ts:

```
@NgModule({
  declarations: [Tooltip, App],
  providers: [Overlay],
```

```
    imports: [BrowserModule],
    bootstrap: [App],
})
class AppModule {}
```

To the @NgModule decorator, we pass an object literal that has the declarations property. This property contains a list of all the directives that will be available in all component subtrees with roots any of the components listed in the bootstrap array. Another way to extend the list of available directives is to import a module. For instance, the module BrowserModule includes some very commonly used directives for the browser environment.

At first, it might seem annoying that you should explicitly declare all the directives that are used in your modules; however, this enforces better encapsulation. In AngularJS, all directives are in a global namespace. This means that all the directives defined in the application are accessible in all the templates. This brings in some problems, for example, name collision. In order to deal with this issue, we introduced naming conventions, for instance, the "ng-" prefix of all the directives defined by AngularJS and "ui-" for all directives coming with the Angular UI.

Currently, by explicitly declaring all the directives that are used within a given module, we create a namespace specific to the individual components' subtrees (that is, the directives will be visible to the given root component and all of its successor components). Preventing name collisions is not the only benefit we get; it also helps us with better semantics of the code that we produce, since we're always aware of the directives accessible by the given component when we know in which module it's declared. We can find all the accessible directives of the given component by following the path from the component to the top module and taking the union of all the values of declarations and the declarations of the modules' imports. Given that components are extended from directives, we need to explicitly declare all the used components as well.

Since Angular defines a set of built-in directives, BrowserModule exports them by exporting the module CommonModule, which contains them. This list of predefined directives includes NgClass, NgFor, NgIf, NgStyle, NgSwitch, NgSwitchWhen, and NgSwitchDefault. Their names are quite self-explanatory; we'll take a look at how we can use some of them later in this chapter.

Using NgModules for declaring reusable components

With NgModules, we can achieve a good degree of encapsulation. By explicitly exporting the public components, directives, pipes, and services, we can hide some of the implementation details of our modules. This way we can implement reusable modules and expose only their public interface, and we do not reveal any low-level components to the user of the module.

In order to get a better idea, let's take a look at the following example:

```
@Component(...)
class ZippyHeader {
  @Input() header: string;
}

@Component(...)
class Zippy {
  @Input() header: string;
  visible = true;
}

@Component(...)
class App {}
```

In the preceding snippet, we declare the components `Zippy`, `ZippyHeader`, and `App`. `Zippy` is a component that has a header and a content; we can toggle the visibility of the content by clicking on the header. In the component `ZippyHeader`, we can implement some logic for handling the click events and/or visualizing the header. In the `App` component, we use the `Zippy` component by passing text for it's header and content.

In order to create a working Angular application, we will need to declare an NgModule, which somehow references all the three components. We can approach this in two main ways:

1. Declare a single NgModule and include all the three components inside of its list of declarations.
2. Declare two NgModules:
   - One that declares the `Zippy` and `ZippyHeader` components, called `ZippyModule`.
   - Another one that declares the `App` component and imports the module `ZippyModule`.

The second approach has a couple of advantages: in `ZippyModule`, we can declare both `Zippy` and `ZippyHeader`, but we can export only `Zippy` because `ZippyHeader` is used internally, within `Zippy`, and we don't have to expose it to the user. By declaring the module `ZippyModule`, we can import it into other modules in our application where we want to reuse the `Zippy` component, or we can even extract it as a separate npm module and reuse it in multiple applications.

The second approach will look like this:

```
// ch4/ts/zippy/app.ts

@Component(...)
class ZippyHeader {...}

@Component(...)
class Zippy {...}

@NgModule({
  declarations: [Zippy, ZippyHeader],
  exports: [Zippy]
  imports: [CommonModule],
})
class ZippyModule {}

@Component(...)
class App {...}

@NgModule({
  imports: [BrowserModule, ZippyModule],
  declarations: [App],
  bootstrap: [App]
})
class AppModule {}

platformBrowserDynamic().bootstrapModule(AppModule);
```

In the preceding example, in the module `ZippyModule`, we declare both `Zippy` and `ZippyHeader`, but we export only `Zippy`. We also import the module `CommonModule` from `@angular/common` in order to reuse Angular's built-in directives (for instance, `NgIf` is exported by the `CommonModule`).

In the `AppModule`, all we need to do is to import `ZippyModule`, and this way, we'll be able to use all of its exports and providers. We'll discuss providers further in the next chapter.

Note that good practices suggest that we should implement each individual component into a separate file. For the sake of simplicity in the examples for this book, we've violated this practice. For a list of best practices, visit `https://angular.io/styleguide`.

Using custom element schema

Now, let's suppose we want to add a timer to our page and reuse a Web Component that we have already built. In this case, our application can look something like this:

```
//  ch4/ts/custom-element/app.ts

import {Component, NgModule} from '@angular/core';
import {BrowserModule} from '@angular/platform-browser';
import {platformBrowserDynamic} from '@angular/platform-browser-dynamic';

@Component({
  selector: 'my-app',
  template: `
    <h1>Hello {{name}}</h1>
    The current timeout is <simple-timer></simple-timer>
  `
})
class App {
  name: string = 'John Doe';
}

@NgModule({
  imports: [BrowserModule],
  declarations: [App],
  bootstrap: [App]
})
class AppModule {}

platformBrowserDynamic().bootstrapModule(AppModule);
```

Now, if we run our application, we'll get the following error:

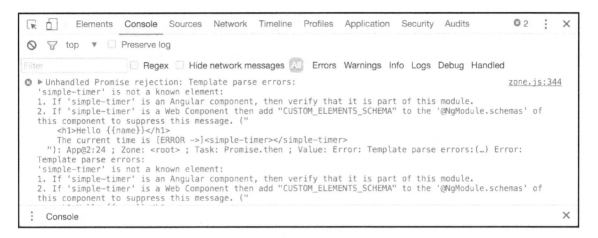

Figure 5

When Angular parses the template of the App component, it will find the `<simple-timer></simple-timer>`. It is not an element defined by the HTML specification and it doesn't match any of the selectors of the directives declared or imported in the `AppModule`, so the framework will throw an error.

So, how we can use Angular with custom components? The solution is to use the `schemas` property of the object literal we pass to `@NgModule`:

```
import {..., CUSTOM_ELEMENTS_SCHEMA} from '@angular/core';

//...

@NgModule({
  imports: [BrowserModule],
  declarations: [App],
  schemas: [CUSTOM_ELEMENTS_SCHEMA],
  bootstrap: [App]
})
class AppModule {}
```

This way we change the default schema that Angular uses for the validation of the elements and their attributes during parsing.

By default, the framework will throw an error if it finds an element that doesn't match the element selector of any of the imported or declared directive, or an element defined by the HTML5 spec.

Creating custom Angular components

Now, let's build a simple to-do application in order to demonstrate the syntax to define components further.

Our to-do items will have the following format:

```
interface Todo {
  completed: boolean;
  label: string;
}
```

Let's start by importing everything we will need:

```
import {Component, NgModule, ViewEncapsulation} from '@angular/core';
//...
```

Now, let's declare the component and the metadata associated with it:

```
@Component({
  selector: 'todo-app',
  templateUrl: './app.html',
  styles: [
    `ul li {
      list-style: none;
    }
    .completed {
      text-decoration: line-through;
    }`
  ],
  encapsulation: ViewEncapsulation.Emulated
})
```

Here, we specify that the selector of the `Todo` component will be the `todo-app` element. Later, we add the template URL, which points to the `app.html` file. After that, we use the `styles` property; this is the first time we encounter it. As we can guess from its name, it is used to set the styles of the component.

Introducing the component's view encapsulation

As we know, Angular is inspired from Web Components, whose core feature is the shadow DOM. The shadow DOM allows us to encapsulate the styles of our Web Components without allowing them to leak outside the component's scope; Angular provides this feature. If we want Angular's renderer to use the shadow DOM, we can use `ViewEncapsulation.Native`. However, at the time of writing this book, the shadow

DOM was not supported by all browsers; if we want to have the same level of encapsulation without using the shadow DOM, we can use `ViewEncapsulation.Emulated`.

If we don't want to have any encapsulation at all, we can use `ViewEncapsulation.None`. By default, the renderer uses encapsulation of the type `Emulated`.

Implementing the component's controllers

Now, let's continue with the implementation of the application:

```
// ch4/ts/todo-app/app.ts
class TodoCtrl {
  todos: Todo[] = [{
    label: 'Buy milk',
    completed: false
  }, {
    label: 'Save the world',
    completed: false
  }];
  name: string = 'John';

  addTodo(label) { ... }

  removeTodo(idx) { ... }

  toggleCompletion(idx) { ... }
}
```

Here is part of the implementation of the controller associated with the template of the `Todo` application. Inside the class declaration, we initialized the `todos` property to an array with two `todo` items.

Now, let's update the template and render these items. Here's how this is done:

```
<ul>
  <li *ngFor="let todo of todos; let index = index"
[class.completed]="todo.completed">
    <input type="checkbox" [checked]="todo.completed"
      (change)="toggleCompletion(index)">
    {{todo.label}}
  </li>
</ul>
```

In the preceding template, we iterate over all the `todo` items inside the `todos` property of the controller. For each `todo` item, we create a checkbox that can `toggle` the item's completion status; we also render the `todo` item's label with the interpolation directive. Here, we can note a syntax that was explained earlier:

- We bind to the change event of the checkbox using `(change)="statement"`.
- We bind to the property of the `todo` item using `[checked]="expr"`.

In order to have a line across the completed `todo` items, we bind to the `class.completed` property of the element. Since we want to apply the `completed` class to all the completed to-do items, we use `[class.completed]="todo.completed"`. This way, we declare that we want to apply the `completed` class depending on the value of the `todo.completed` expression. Here is how our application looks now:

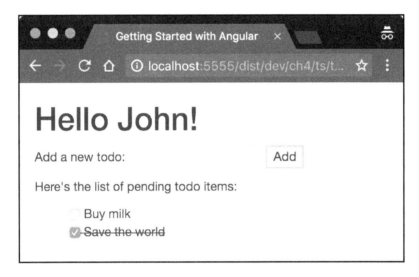

Figure 6

 Similar to the class binding syntax, Angular allows us to bind to the element's styles and attributes. For instance, we can bind to the `td` element's `colspan` attribute using the following line of code:
`<td [attr.colspan]="colspanCount"></td>`
In the same way, we can bind to any `style` property using this line of code: `<div [style.backgroundImage]="expression"></td>`

Handling user actions

So far, so good! Now, let's implement the `toggleCompletion` method. This method accepts the index of the to-do item as an argument:

```
toggleCompletion(idx) {
  let todo = this.todos[idx];
  todo.completed = !todo.completed;
}
```

In `toggleCompletion`, we simply toggle the `completed` boolean value associated with the current to-do item, which is specified by the index passed as an argument to the method.

Now, let's add a text input to add the new to-do items:

```
<p>
  Add a new todo:
  <input #newtodo type="text">
  <button (click)="addTodo(newtodo.value); newtodo.value = ''">
    Add
  </button>
</p>
```

The input here defines a new variable called `newtodo`. Now, we can reference the input element using the `newtodo` identifier inside the template. Once the user clicks on the button, the `addTodo` method defined in the controller will be invoked with the value of the `newtodo` input as an argument. Inside the statement that is passed to the `(click)` attribute, we also reset the value of the `newtodo` input by setting it to the empty string.

 Note that directly manipulating DOM elements is not considered as the best practice since it will prevent our component from running properly outside the browser environment. We will explain how we can migrate this application to Web Workers in `Chapter 8`, *Tooling and Development Experience*.

Now, let's define the `addTodo` method:

```
addTodo(label) {
  this.todos.push({
    label,
    completed: false
  });
}
```

Inside it, we create a new to-do item using the object literal syntax.

The only thing left out of our application is to implement removal of the existing to-do items. Since it is quite similar to the functionality used to toggle the completion of the to-do items, I'll leave its implementation as a simple exercise for the reader.

Using inputs and outputs

By refactoring our `todo` application, we will demonstrate how we can take advantage of the directives' inputs and outputs:

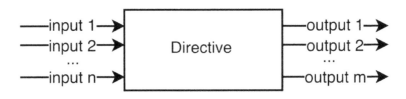

Figure 7

We can think of the inputs as properties (or even arguments) that the given directive accepts. The outputs could be considered as events that it triggers. When we use a directive provided by a third-party library, mostly, we care about its inputs and outputs because they define its API.

Inputs refer to values that parameterize the directive's behavior and/or view. On the other hand, outputs refer to events that the directive fires when something special happens.

Determining of the inputs and outputs

Now, let's divide our monolithic to-do application into separate components that communicate with each other. In the following screenshot, you can see the individual components, which when composed together, implement the functionality of the application:

Figure 8

The outer rectangle represents the entire `Todo` application. The first nested rectangle contains the component that is responsible for entering labels of the new to-do items, and the one below it lists the individual items stored in the root component.

Having said this, we can define these three components as follows:

- `TodoApp`: This is responsible for maintaining the list of to-do items (adding new items and toggling the completion status).
- `InputBox`: This is responsible for entering the label of the new to-do item. It has the following inputs and outputs:
  - Inputs: a placeholder for the textbox and a label for the submit button.
  - Outputs: the content of the textbox once the submit button is clicked.
- `TodoList`: This is responsible for rendering the individual to-do items. It has the following inputs and outputs:
  - Inputs: a list of to-do items.
  - Outputs: the completion status of a to-do item.

Now, let's begin with the implementation!

Defining the inputs and outputs

Let's use a bottom-up approach, and start with the `InputBox` component. Before that, we need a couple of imports from Angular's `@angular/core` package:

```
import {
  Component,
  Input,
  Output,
  EventEmitter
} from '@angular/core';
```

In the preceding code, we import the `@Component`, `@Input`, and `@Output` decorators and the `EventEmitter` class. As their names state, `@Input` and `@Output` are used for declaring the directive's inputs and outputs. `EventEmitter` is a generic class (that is, accepting a type parameter), which when combined with the `@Output` decorator helps us emit outputs.

As the next step, let's take a look at the `InputBox` component's declaration:

```
// ch4/ts/inputs-outputs/app.ts

@Component({
  selector: 'text-input',
  template: `
    <input #todoInput [placeholder]="inputPlaceholder">
    <button (click)="emitText(todoInput.value);
                      todoInput.value = '';">
      {{buttonLabel}}
    </button>
    `
})
class InputBox {...}
```

Note that in the template, we declare a text input and keep a reference to it using the `todoInput` identifier, and set its placeholder property to the value that we got from the evaluation of the `inputPlaceholder` expression. The value of the expression is the value of the `inputPlaceholder` property defined in the component's controller. This is the first input that we need to declare:

```
class InputBox {
  @Input() inputPlaceholder: string;
  ...
}
```

Similarly, we declare the other input of the `buttonLabel` component, which we use as a value of the label of the button:

```
class InputBox {
  @Input() inputPlaceholder: string;
  @Input() buttonLabel: string;
  ...
}
```

In the preceding template, we bind the click event of the button to this `emitText(todoInput.value); todoInput.value = '';` statement. The `emitText` method should be defined in the component's controller; once it is invoked, it should emit the value of the text input. Here is how we can implement this behavior:

```
class InputBox {
  ...
  @Output() inputText = new EventEmitter<string>();

  emitText(text: string) {
    this.inputText.emit(text);
  }
}
```

Initially, we declare an output called `inputText`. As its value, we set a new instance of the type `EventEmitter<string>` that we create.

 Note that all the outputs of all the components need to be instances of `EventEmitter`.

Inside the `emitText` method, we invoke the `emit` method of the `inputText` and as its argument we pass the value of the text input.

Now, let's define the `TodoList` component in the same fashion:

```
@Component(...)
class TodoList {
  @Input() todos: Todo[];
  @Output() toggle = new EventEmitter<Todo>();

  toggleCompletion(index: number) {
    let todo = this.todos[index];
    this.toggle.emit(todo);
  }
}
```

Since the value of the object literal passed to the `@Component` decorator is not essential for the purpose of this section, we omitted it. The complete implementation of this example can be found at `ch4/ts/inputs-outputs/app.ts`. Let's take a look at the body of the `TodoList` class. Similarly, to the `InputBox` component, we define the `todos` input. We also define the `toggle` output by declaring the `toggle` property, setting its value to a new instance of the type `EventEmitter<Todo>` and decorating it with the `@Output` decorator.

Passing inputs and consuming the outputs

Now, let's combine the components we defined in the preceding section and implement our complete application.

The last component we need to take a look at is `TodoApp`:

```
@Component({
  selector: 'todo-app',
  template: `
    <h1>Hello {{name}}!</h1>

    <p>
      Add a new todo:
      <input-box inputPlaceholder="New todo..."
        buttonLabel="Add"
        (inputText)="addTodo($event)">
      </input-box>
    </p>

    <p>Here's the list of pending todo items:</p>
    <todo-list [todos]="todos" (toggle)="toggleCompletion($event)"></todo-list>
    `
})
class TodoApp {...}
```

Initially, we define the `TodoApp` class and decorate it with the `@Component` decorator. Note that in order to use the `InputBox` and `TodoList` components, we will need to include them in the `declarations` property of the decorator of the module, which declares `TodoApp`. The magic of how these components collaborate together happens in the template:

```
<input-box inputPlaceholder="New todo..."
  buttonLabel="Add"
  (inputText)="addTodo($event)">
</input-box>
```

First, we use the `InputBox` component and pass values to the inputs `inputPlaceholder` and `buttonLabel`. Note that just like we saw earlier, if we want to pass an expression as a value to any of these inputs, we will need to surround them with brackets (that is, `[inputPlaceholder]="expression"`). In this case, the expression will be evaluated in the context of the component that owns the template, and the result will be passed as an input to the component that owns the given property.

Right after we pass the value for the `buttonLabel` input, we consume the `inputText` output by setting the value of the `(inputText)` attribute to the `addTodo($event)` expression. *The value of* `$event` *will equal the value we passed to the* `emit` *method of the* `inputText` *object inside the* `emitText` *method of* `InputBox` (in case we bind to a native event, the value of the event object will be the native event object itself).

In the same way, we pass the input of the `TodoList` component and handle its toggle output. Now, let's define the logic behind the `TodoApp` component:

```
class TodoApp {
  todos: Todo[] = [];
  name: string = 'John';

  addTodo(label: string) {
    this.todos.push({
      label,
      completed: false
    });
  }

  toggleCompletion(todo: Todo) {
    todo.completed = !todo.completed;
  }
}
```

In the `addTodo` method, we simply push a new to-do item to the `todos` array. The implementation of `toggleCompletion` is even simpler: we toggle the value of the completed flag that is passed as an argument to the to-do item. Now, we are familiar with the basics of the components' inputs and outputs.

Event bubbling

In Angular, we have the same bubbling behavior we're used to in the DOM. For instance, let's suppose we have the following template:

```
<input-box inputPlaceholder="New todo..."
```

```
    buttonLabel="Add"
    (click)="handleClick($event)"
    (inputText)="addTodo($event)">
</input-box>
```

The declaration of `input-box` looks like this:

```
<input #todoInput [placeholder]="inputPlaceholder">
<button (click)="emitText(todoInput.value);
                 todoInput.value = '';">
  {{buttonLabel}}
</button>
```

Once the user clicks on the button defined within the template of the `input-box` component, the `handleClick($event)` expression will be evaluated.

Further, the `target` property of the first argument of `handleClick` will be the button itself, but the `currentTarget` property will be the `input-box` element. The event will bubble the same way if we're not using Angular. At some point, it will reach the document unless a handler along the way doesn't stop its propagation.

In contrast, if we have a custom `@Output`, the event will not bubble and instead of a DOM event, the value of the `$event` variable will be the value that we pass to the emit method of the output.

Renaming the inputs and outputs

Now, we will explore how we can rename the directives' inputs and outputs. Let's suppose that we have the following definition of the `TodoList` component:

```
class TodoList {
  ...
  @Output() toggle = new EventEmitter<Todo>();

  toggle(index: number) {
    ...
  }
}
```

The output of the component is called `toggle`; the method that handles changes in the checkboxes responsible for toggling completion of the individual to-do items is also called `toggle`. This code will not be compiled, as in the `TodoList` controller we have two identifiers named in the same way. We have two options here:

- We can rename the method.
- We can rename the property.

If we rename the property, this will change the name of the component's output as well. So, the following line of code will no longer work:

```
<todo-list [toggle]="foobar($event)"...></todo-list>
```

What we can do instead is rename the `toggle` property and explicitly set the name of the output using the `@Output` decorator:

```
class TodoList {
  ...
  @Output('toggle') toggleEvent = new EventEmitter<Todo>();

  toggle(index: number) {
    ...
  }
}
```

This way, we will be able to trigger the `toggle` output using the `toggleEvent` property.

> Note that such renames could be confusing and are not considered as best practices. For a complete set of best practices, visit `https://angular.io/styleguide`.

Similarly, we can rename the component's inputs using the following code snippet:

```
class TodoList {
  @Input('todos') todoList: Todo[];
  @Output('toggle') toggleEvent = new EventEmitter<Todo>();

  toggle(index: number) {
    ...
  }
}
```

Now, it doesn't matter that we renamed the input and output properties of `TodoList`; it still has the same public interface:

```
<todo-list [todos]="todos"
  (toggle)="toggleCompletion($event)">
</todo-list>
```

An alternative syntax to define inputs and outputs

The `@Input` and `@Output` decorators are syntax sugar for easier declaration of the directive's inputs and outputs. The original syntax for this purpose is as follows:

```
@Directive({
  outputs: ['outputName: outputAlias'],
  inputs: ['inputName: inputAlias']
})
class Dir {
  outputName = new EventEmitter();
}
```

Using `@Input` and `@Output`, the preceding syntax is equivalent to this:

```
@Directive(...)
class Dir {
  @Output('outputAlias') outputName = new EventEmitter<any>();
  @Input('inputAlias') inputName: any;
}
```

Although both have the same semantics, according to the best practices, we should use the latter one, because it is easier to read and understand.

Explaining Angular's content projection

Content projection is an important concept when developing user interfaces. It allows us to project pieces of content into different places of the user interface of our application. Web Components solve this problem with the `content` element. In AngularJS, it is implemented with the infamous transclusion.

Angular is inspired by modern Web standards, especially Web Components, which led to the adoption of some of the methods of content projection used there. In this section, we'll look at them in the context of Angular using the `ng-content` directive.

Basic content projection in Angular

Let's suppose we're building a component called `fancy-button`. This component will use the standard HTML button element and add some extra behavior to it. Here is the definition of the `fancy-button` component:

```
@Component({
  selector: 'fancy-button',
  template: '<button>Click me</button>'
})
class FancyButton { ... }
```

Inside of the `@Component` decorator, we set the inline template of the component together with its selector. Now, we can use the component with the following markup:

```
<fancy-button></fancy-button>
```

On the screen, we will see a standard HTML button that has a label with the content **Click me**. This is not a very flexible way to define reusable UI components. Most likely, the users of the fancy button will need to change the content of the label to something, depending on their application.

In AngularJS, we were able to achieve this result with `ng-transclude`:

```
// AngularJS example
app.directive('fancyButton', function () {
  return {
    restrict: 'E',
    transclude: true,
    template: '<button><ng-transclude></ng-transclude></button>'
  };
});
```

In the new Angular, we have the `ng-content` element:

```
// ch4/ts/ng-content/app.ts
@Component({
  selector: 'fancy-button',
  template: '<button><ng-content></ng-content></button>'
})
class FancyButton { /* Extra behavior */ }
```

Now, we can pass custom content to the fancy button by executing this:

```
<fancy-button>Click <i>me</i> now!</fancy-button>
```

As a result, the content between the opening and the closing `fancy-button` tags will be placed where the `ng-content` directive resides.

Projecting multiple content chunks

Another typical use case of content projection is when we pass content to a custom Angular component or AngularJS directive and we want different parts of this content to be projected to different locations in the template.

For instance, let's suppose we have a `panel` component that has a title and a body, and we can use it in the following way:

```
<panel>
  <section class="panel-title">Sample title</section>
  <section class="panel-content">Content</section>
</panel>
```

The template of our `panel` component looks like this:

```
<div class="panel">
  <div class="panel-title">
    <!-- Project the content of panel-title here -->
  </div>
  <div class="panel-content">
    <!-- Project the content of panel-content here -->
  </div>
</div>`
```

In AngularJS 1.5, we are able to do this using multi-slot transclusion, which was implemented in order to allow us to have a smoother transition to Angular 2 and later versions. Let's take a look at how we can proceed in Angular in order to define such a `panel` component:

```
// ch4/ts/ng-content/app.ts
@Component({
  selector: 'panel',
  styles: [ ... ],
  template: `
    <div class="panel">
      <div class="panel-title">
        <ng-content select=".panel-title"></ng-content>
```

```
    </div>
    <div class="panel-content">
      <ng-content select=".panel-content"></ng-content>
    </div>
  </div>`
})
class Panel { }
```

We have already described the `selector` and `styles` properties, so let's take a look at the component's template. We have a `div` element with the `panel` class, which wraps the two nested `div` elements, respectively — one for the title of `panel` and one for the content of `panel`.

In order to project the content of the `section` element with class name `panel-title` to where the title should be, we will need to use the `ng-content` element. As its `selector` attribute, we will need to use a CSS selector, which matches the element whose content we want to project (in this case, the selector should be `.panel-title` or `section.panel-title`).

In case we set the value of the `selector` attribute to `.panel-title`, it will match all the elements with classes `.panel-title` that reside inside the target `panel` element. After this, `ng-content` will grab their content and set them as its own content.

Nesting components

We've already built a few simple applications as a composition of components and directives. We saw that components are basically directives with views, so we can implement them by nesting or composing other directives and components. The following figure illustrates this with a structural diagram:

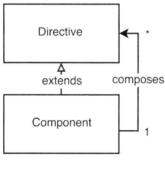

Figure 9

The composition could be achieved by nesting directives and components within the components' templates, taking advantage of the nested nature of the used markup. For instance, let's say we have a component with the `sample-component` selector, which has the following definition:

```
@Component({
  selector: 'sample-component',
  template: '<view-child></view-child>'
})
class Sample {}
```

The template of the `Sample` component has a single-child element with the tag name `view-child`.

On the other hand, we can use the `Sample` component inside the template of another component, and since it can be used as an element, we can also nest other components or directives inside of it:

```
<sample-component>
  <content-child1></content-child1>
  <content-child2></content-child2>
</sample-component>
```

This way, the `sample-component` component has two different types of successors:

- Successors defined within its template.
- Successors passed as nested elements between its opening and closing tags.

In the context of Angular, the direct children elements defined within the component's template are called **view children** and the ones nested between its opening and closing tags are called **content children**.

Using ViewChildren and ContentChildren

Let's take a look at the implementation of the `Tabs` component, which uses the following structure:

```
<tabs (changed)="tabChanged($event)">
  <tab-title>Tab 1</tab-title>
  <tab-content>Content 1</tab-content>
  <tab-title>Tab 2</tab-title>
  <tab-content>Content 2</tab-content>
</tabs>
```

The preceding structure is composed of three components:

- `Tab` component
- `TabTitle` component
- `TabContent` component

Let's take a look at the implementation of the `TabTitle` component:

```
@Component({
  selector: 'tab-title',
  styles: [...],
  template: `
    <div class="tab-title" (click)="handleClick()">
      <ng-content></ng-content>
    </div>
  `
})
class TabTitle {
  @Output() tabSelected: EventEmitter<TabTitle> =
    new EventEmitter<TabTitle>();

  handleClick() {
    this.tabSelected.emit(this);
  }
}
```

There's nothing new in this implementation. We define a `TabTitle` component, which has a single property called `tabSelected`. It is of the type `EventEmitter` and will be triggered once the user clicks on the tab title.

Now, let's take a look at the `TabContent` component:

```
@Component({
  selector: 'tab-content',
  styles: [...],
  template: `
    <div class="tab-content" [hidden]="!isActive">
      <ng-content></ng-content>
    </div>
  `
})
class TabContent {
  isActive: boolean = false;
}
```

This has an even simpler implementation — all we do is project the DOM passed to the `tab-content` element inside `ng-content` and hide it once the value of the `isActive` property becomes `false`.

The interesting part of the implementation is the `Tabs` component itself:

```
// ch4/ts/basic-tab-content-children/app.ts
@Component({
  selector: 'tabs',
  styles: [...],
  template: `
    <div class="tab">
      <div class="tab-nav">
        <ng-content select="tab-title"></ng-content>
      </div>
      <ng-content select="tab-content"></ng-content>
    </div>
  `
})
class Tabs {
  @Output('changed')
  tabChanged: EventEmitter<number> = new EventEmitter<number>();

  @ContentChildren(TabTitle)
  tabTitles: QueryList<TabTitle>;

  @ContentChildren(TabContent)
  tabContents: QueryList<TabContent>;

  active: number;
  select(index: number) {...}
  ngAfterViewInit() {...}
}
```

In this implementation, we have a decorator that we haven't used yet: the `@ContentChildren` decorator. The `@ContentChildren` property decorator fetches the content children of the given component. This means that we can get references to all `TabTitle` and `TabContent` instances from within the instance of the `Tabs` component and get them in the order in which they are declared in the markup. There's an alternative decorator called `@ViewChildren`, which fetches all the view children of the given element. Let's take a look at the difference between view children versus content children before we explain the implementation further.

ViewChild versus ContentChild

Although both concepts sound similar, they have quite different semantics. In order to understand them better, let's take a look at the following example:

```
// ch4/ts/view-child-content-child/app.ts
@Component({
  selector: 'user-badge',
  template: '...'
})
class UserBadge {}

@Component({
  selector: 'user-rating',
  template: '...'
})
class UserRating {}
```

Here, we've defined two components: `UserBadge` and `UserRating`. Let's define a parent component, which comprises both the components:

```
@Component({
  selector: 'user-panel',
  template: '<user-badge></user-badge>'
})
class UserPanel {...}
```

Note that the template of the view of `UserPanel` contains only the `UserBadge` component's selector. Now, let's use the `UserPanel` component in our application:

```
@Component({
  selector: 'app',
  template: `<user-panel>
    <user-rating></user-rating>
  </user-panel>`
})
class App {}
```

The template of our main `App` component uses the `UserPanel` component and nests the `UserRating` component inside it. Now, let's suppose we want to get a reference to the instance of the `UserRating` component that is used inside the `user-panel` element in the `App`'s template and a reference to the `UserBadge` component, which is used inside the `UserPanel`'s template. In order to do this, we can add two more properties to the `UserPanel` controller and add the `@ContentChild` and `@ViewChild` decorators to them with the appropriate arguments:

```
class UserPanel {
  @ViewChild(UserBadge)
  badge: UserBadge;

  @ContentChild(UserRating)
  rating: UserRating;

  constructor() {
    //
  }
}
```

The semantics of the `badge` property declaration is "get the instance of the first child component of the type `UserBadge`, which is used inside the `UserPanel` template". Accordingly, the semantics of the `rating` property's declaration is "get the instance of the first child component of the type `UserRating`, which is nested inside the `UserPanel` host element".

Now, if you run this code, you'll note that the values of the `badge` and `rating` properties are still equal to the `undefined` value inside the controller's constructor. This is because they are still not initialized in this phase of the component's life cycle. The life cycle hooks that we can use in order to get a reference to these child components are `ngAfterViewInit` and `ngAfterContentInit`. We can use these hooks simply by adding definitions of the `ngAfterViewInit` and `ngAfterContentInit` methods to the component's controller. We will make a complete overview of the life cycle hooks that Angular provides shortly.

To recap, we can say that the content children of the given components are the child elements that are nested within the component's host element. In contrast, the view children directives of the given component are the elements used within its template.

 In order to get a platform independent reference to a DOM element, again, we can use `@ContentChild` and `@ViewChild`. For instance, if we have the following template: `<input #todo>` we can get a reference to the `input` by using: `@ViewChild('todo')`.

Since we are already familiar with the core differences between view children and content children now, we can continue with our tabs implementation.

In the tabs component, instead of using the `@ContentChild` decorator, we use `@ContentChildren`. We do this because we have multiple content children and we want to get them all:

```
@ContentChildren(TabTitle)
tabTitles: QueryList<TabTitle>;

@ContentChildren(TabContent)
tabContents: QueryList<TabContent>;
```

Another main difference that we will note is that the types of the `tabTitles` and `tabContents` properties are `QueryList` with their respective type parameter and not the component's type itself. We can think of the `QueryList` data structure as a JavaScript array — we can apply the same high-order functions (`map`, `filter`, `reduce`, and so on) over it and loop over its elements; however, `QueryList` is also observable, that is, we can observe it for changes.

As the final step of our `Tabs` definition, let's take a peek at the implementation of the `ngAfterContentInit` and `select` methods:

```
ngAfterContentInit() {
  this.tabTitles
    .map(t => t.tabSelected)
    .forEach((t, i) => {
      t.subscribe(_ => {
        this.select(i)
      });
    });
  this.active = 0;
  this.select(0);
}
```

In the first line of the method's implementation, we loop all `tabTitles` and take the observable's references. These objects have a method called `subscribe`, which accepts a callback as an argument. Once the `.emit()` method of the `EventEmitter` instance (that is, the `tabSelected` property of any tab) is called, the callback passed to the `subscribe` method will be invoked.

Now, let's take a look at the `select` method's implementation:

```
select(index: number) {
  let contents: TabContent[] = this.tabContents.toArray();
  contents[this.active].isActive = false;
  this.active = index;
  contents[this.active].isActive = true;
  this.tabChanged.emit(index);
}
```

In the first line, since `tabContents` is of the type `QueryList<TabContent>`, we get its array representation. After that, we set the `isActive` flag of the current active tab to `false` and select the next active one. In the last line in the `select` method's implementation, we trigger the selected event of the `Tabs` component by invoking `this.tabChanged.emit` with the index of the currently selected tab.

Hooking into the component's life cycle

Components in Angular have a well-defined life cycle, which allows us to hook into different phases of it and have further control over our application. We can do this by implementing specific methods in the component's controller. In order to be more explicit, thanks to the expressiveness of TypeScript, we can implement different interfaces associated with the life cycle's phases. Each of these interfaces has a single method, which is associated with the phase itself.

Although code written with explicit interface implementation will have better semantics, since Angular supports ES5 as well, within the component we can simply define methods with the same names as the life cycle hooks (but this time, prefixed with `ng`) and take advantage of duck typing.

The following diagram shows all the phases we can hook into:

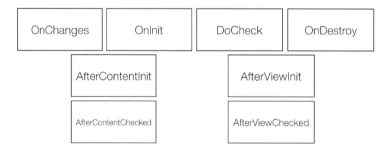

Figure 10

Let's take a look at the different life cycle hooks:

- `OnChanges`: This hook will be invoked once a change in the input properties of a given component is detected. For instance, let's take a look at the following component:

```
@Component({
    selector: 'panel',
    inputs: ['title']
})
class Panel {...}
```

We can use it like this:

```
<panel [title]="expression"></panel>
```

Once the value of the expression associated with the `[title]` attribute is changed, the `ngOnChanges` hook will be invoked. We can implement it using this code snippet:

```
@Component(...)
class Panel {
  ngOnChanges(changes) {
    Object.keys(changes).forEach(prop => {
      console.log(prop, 'changed. Previous value',
changes[prop].previousValue);
    });
  }
}
```

The preceding snippet will display all the changed bindings and their old values. In order to be more explicit in the implementation of the hook, we can use interfaces:

```
import {Component, OnChanges} from '@angular/core';
@Component(...)
class Panel implements OnChanges {
  ngOnChanges(changes) {...}
}
```

All the interfaces representing the individual life cycle hooks declare a single method with the name of the interface itself prefixed with `ng`. In the upcoming list, we'll use the term life cycle hook, both for interface and/or the method, except if we won't imply anything specifically for only one of them.

- `OnInit`: This hook will be invoked once the given component is initialized. We can implement it using the `OnInit` interface with its `ngOnInit` method.

- `DoCheck`: This will be invoked when the change detector of the given component is invoked. It allows us to implement our own change detection algorithm for the given component. Note that `DoCheck` and `OnChanges` should not be implemented together on the same directive.
- `OnDestroy`: If we implement the `OnDestroy` interface with its `ngOnDestroy` method, we can hook into the destroy life cycle phase of a component. This method will be invoked once the component is detached from the component tree.

Now, let's take a look at the life cycle hooks associated with the component's content and view children:

- `AfterContentInit`: If we implement the `ngAfterContentInit` life cycle hook, we will be notified when the component's content is fully initialized. This is the phase when the properties decorated with `ContentChild` or `ContentChildren` will be initialized.
- `AfterContentChecked`: By implementing this hook, we'll be notified each time the content of the given component has been checked by the change detection mechanism of Angular.
- `AfterViewInit`: If we implement this life cycle hook with its `ngAfterViewInit` method, we will be notified when the component's view is initialized. This is the phase when the properties decorated with `ViewChild` or `ViewChildren` will be initialized.
- `AfterViewChecked`: This is similar to `AfterContentChecked`. The `AfterViewChecked` hook will be invoked once the view of our component is checked.

Order of execution of the life cycle hooks

In order to trace the order of execution of the callbacks associated with each hook, let's take a peek at the `ch4/ts/life-cycle/app.ts` example:

```
@Component({
  selector: 'panel',
  template: '<ng-content></ng-content>'
})
class Panel {
  @Input() title: string;
  @Input() caption: string;
  ngOnChanges(changes) {...}
  ngOnInit() {...}
```

```
    ngDoCheck() {...}
    ngOnDestroy() {...}
    ngAfterContentInit() {...}
    ngAfterContentChecked() {...}
    ngAfterViewInit() {...}
    ngAfterViewChecked() {...}
}
```

The `Panel` component implements all the hooks without explicitly implementing the interfaces associated with them.

We can use the component in the following template:

```
<button (click)="toggle()">Toggle</button>
<div *ngIf="counter % 2 == 0">
  <panel caption="Sample caption" >Hello world!</panel>
</div>
```

In the preceding example, we have a panel and a button. Upon each click of the button, the panel will be either removed or appended to the view by the `ngIf` directive.

During the application initialization, if the result of the `"counter % 2 == 0"` expression is evaluated to `true`, the `ngOnChanges` method will be invoked. This happens because the values of the title and caption properties will be set for the first time.

Right after this, the `ngOnInit` method will be called, since the component has been initialized. Once the component's initialization is completed, the change detection will be triggered, which will lead to the invocation of the `ngDoCheck` method that allows us to hook custom logic for detecting changes in the state.

Note that you are not supposed to implement both `ngDoCheck` and `ngOnChanges` methods for the same component, since `ngOnChanges` will keep being called when the internal change detector detects changes. The example here does this for learning purposes only.

After the `ngDoCheck` method, the change detector will perform a check on the component's content (`ngAfterContentInit` and `ngAfterContentChecked` will be invoked in this order). Right after this, the same will happen for the component's view (`ngAfterViewInit` followed by `ngAfterViewChecked`).

Once the expression of the `ngIf` directive is evaluated to `false`, the entire component will be detached from the view, which will lead to the invocation of the `ngOnDestroy` hook.

On the next click, if the value of the expression of ngIf is equal to true, the same sequence of calls of the life cycle hooks as the one during the initialization phase will be executed.

Defining generic views with TemplateRef

We are already familiar with the concepts of inputs, content children, and view children, and we also know when we can get a reference to them in the component's life cycle. Now, we will combine them and introduce a new concept–TemplateRef.

Let's take a step back and take a look at the last to-do application we developed earlier in this chapter. In the following screenshot, you can see what its UI looks like:

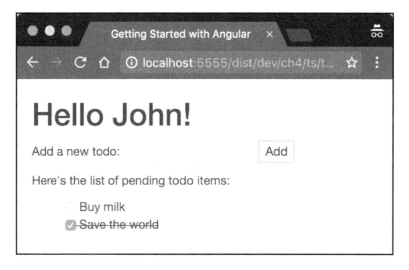

Figure 11

If we take a look at its implementation in ch4/ts/inputs-outputs/app.ts, we'll see that the template used to render the individual to-do items is defined inside the template of the entire to-do application.

What if we want to use a different layout to render the to-do items? We can do this by creating another component called Todo, which encapsulates the responsibility of rendering them. Then, we can define separate Todo components for the different layouts we want to support. This way, we need to have *n* different components for *n* different layouts, even though we need to change only their templates.

Angular comes with a more elegant solution. Earlier in this chapter, we have already discussed the template element. We said that it allows us to define a chunk of HTML that will not be processed by the browser. Angular allows us to reference such template elements and use them by passing them as content children.

Here is how we can pass the custom layout to our refactored `TodoApp` component:

```
// ch4/ts/template-ref/app.ts
<todo-app>
  <template let-todo>
    <input type="checkbox" [checked]="todo.completed"
      (change)="todo.completed = !todo.completed;">
    <span [class.completed]="todo.completed">
      {{todo.label}}
    </span><br>
  </template>
</todo-app>
```

In the template, we declare a variable called `todo`. Later in the template, we can use it to specify the way in which we want to visualize the content.

Now, let's take a look at how we can get a reference to this template in the controller of the `TodoApp` component:

```
// ch4/ts/template-ref/app.ts
class TodoApp {
  @ContentChild(TemplateRef) itemsTemplate: TemplateRef;
  // ...
}
```

All we do here is define a property called `itemsTemplate` and decorate it with the `@ContentChild` decorator. During the component's life cycle (more accurately, in `ngAfterContentInit`), the value of `itemsTemplate` will be set to a reference of the template that we passed as the content of the `todo-app` element.

There is one more problem though — we need the template in the `TodoList` component, since that's the place where we render the individual to-do items. What we can do is define another input of the `TodoList` component and pass the template directly from `TodoApp`:

```
// ch4/ts/template-ref/app.ts
class TodoList {
  @Input() todos: Todo[];
  @Input() itemsTemplate: TemplateRef;
  @Output() toggle = new EventEmitter<Todo>();
}
```

We need to pass it as an input from the template of `TodoApp`:

```
...
<todo-list [todos]="todos"
  [itemsTemplate]="itemsTemplate">
</todo-list>
```

The only thing left is to use this template reference in the template of the `TodoList` application:

```
<!-- ... -->
<template *ngFor="let todo of todos; template: itemsTemplate"></template>
```

We have explained the extended syntax of the `ngForOf` directive in the previous sections of this chapter. The preceding snippet shows one more property of this directive that we can set: the `ngForTemplate` property. By default, the template of the `ngForOf` directive is the element it is used on. By specifying a template reference to the `ngForTemplate` property, we can use the passed `TemplateRef` instead.

Understanding and enhancing the change detection

We have already briefly described the change detection mechanism of the framework. We said that compared to AngularJS, where it runs in the context of the "scope", in Angular 2 and later versions, it runs in the context of the individual components. Another concept we mentioned is the zones, which basically intercept all the asynchronous calls that we make using the browser APIs and provide execution context for the change detection mechanism of the framework. Zones fix the annoying problem that we have in AngularJS, where when we use APIs outside of Angular, we needed to explicitly invoke the `digest` loop.

In `Chapter 1`, *Get Going with Angular* and `Chapter 2`, *The Building Blocks of an Angular Application*, we discussed that the code that performs change detection over our components is being generated, either runtime (**Just-in-Time**) or as part of our build process (**Ahead-of-Time**). AoT compilation works great for environments with strict **CSP** (**Content-Security-Policy**) because of the disabled dynamic evaluation of JavaScript; it also provides much better performance since Angular will not have to compile the components' templates. We will explain it in detail in `Chapter 8`, *Tooling and Development Experience*.

In this section, we'll explore another property of the @Component decorator's configuration object, which provides us further control over the change detection mechanism of the framework by changing its strategy. By explicitly setting the strategy, we are able to prevent the change detection mechanism from running over a component's subtrees, which in some cases can bring great performance benefits.

The order of execution of the change detectors

Now, let's briefly describe the order in which the change detectors are invoked in a given component tree.

For this purpose, we will use the last implementation of the to-do application we have, but this time, we'll extract the logic to render the individual to-do items into a separate component called TodoItem. In the following diagram, we can see the application's structure:

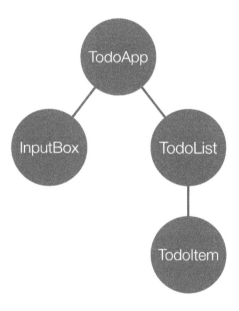

Figure 12

At the top level is the **TodoApp** component, which has two children: **InputBox** and **TodoList**. The **TodoList** component renders the individual to-do items using the **TodoItem** components. The implementation details are not important for our purpose, so we will ignore them.

Now, we need to realize that there is an implicit dependency between the state of the parent component and its children. For instance, the state of the **TodoList** component depends completely on the to-do items that are located at its parent: the **TodoApp** component. There's a similar dependency between **TodoItem** and **TodoList** since the **TodoList** component passes the individual to-do items to a separate instance of the **TodoItem** component. This means that if the list of to-do items in **TodoList** changes, this will automatically reflect some of the **TodoItem** components:

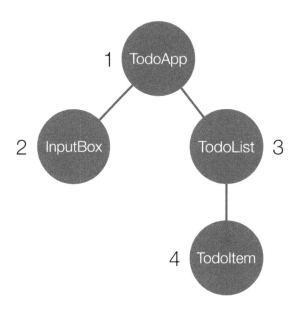

Figure 13

Owing to our last observation, the order of execution of the change detectors attached to the individual components is like the one shown in the preceding figure. Once the change detection mechanism run, initially it will perform a check over the **TodoApp** component. Right after this, the **InputBox** component will be checked for changes, followed by the **TodoList** component. In the end, Angular will invoke the change detector of the **TodoItem** component.

You can trace the order of execution in the `ch4/ts/change_detection_strategy_order/app.ts` example, where each individual component logs a message once its `ngDoCheck` method is invoked.

Note that only the components have an instance of a change detector attached to them; directives use the change detector of their parent component.

Understanding Angular's change detection strategies

The change detection strategies that Angular provides are `Default` and `OnPush`. We will describe how we can take advantage of `OnPush` in detail, since it is very powerful when working with immutable data.

Now, let's import the TypeScript enum, which can be used to configure the strategy used for the individual components:

```
// ch4/ts/change_detection_strategy_broken/app.ts

import {ChangeDetectionStrategy} from '@angular/core';
```

Now, we can configure the `TodoList` component to use the `OnPush` strategy:

```
@Component({
  selector: 'todo-list',
  changeDetection: ChangeDetectionStrategy.OnPush,
  template: `...`,
  styles: [...]
})
class TodoList { ... }
```

This way, the change detection will be skipped until the component doesn't receive inputs that have different values. Note that comparison uses equality check, which means that it'll compare primitive types by their value and objects by comparing their references. You can go to `http://localhost:5555/dist/dev/ch4/ts/change_detection_strategy_broken/` and see the inconsistent behavior of the `TodoList` component. When you add a new to-do item in the input and click on the **Add** button, it won't immediately appear in the list.

By default, the change detection will always check for changes.

Introducing immutable data structures and OnPush

Now, we will describe the OnPush change detection strategy. It is extremely useful when the result that the given component produces depends only on its inputs. In such cases, we can pass an immutable data to its inputs in order to make sure that it will not be mutated by any component. This way, by having a component that depends only on its immutable inputs and doesn't produce any side effects, we can make sure that it produces different user interfaces only once it receives different inputs (that is, with different reference).

In this section, we will apply the OnPush strategy to the TodoList component. Since it depends only on its inputs (the todos input), we want to make sure that its change detection will be performed only once it receives a new reference of the todos collection.

The essence of an immutable data is that it cannot change. This means that once we create the todos collection, we cannot change it; instead, the add (or, in our case, push) method will return a new collection–a copy of the initial collection with the new item included.

This may seem like a huge overhead–to copy the entire collection on each change. In big applications, this may have a big performance impact. However, we don't need to copy the entire collection. There are libraries that implement the immutable data structure using smarter algorithms, for example, persistent data structures. Persistent data structures are out of the scope of the current content. Further information about them can be found in most computer science textbooks for advanced data structures. The good thing is that we don't have to understand their implementation in depth in order to use them. There is a library called *Immutable.js* that implements a few commonly used immutable data structures. In our case, we will use the immutable list. Generally, the immutable list behaves just like a normal list, but on each operation that is supposed to mutate it, it returns a new immutable list.

This means that if we have a list called foo, which is immutable, and append a new item to the list, we will get a new reference:

```
let foo = List.of(1, 2, 3);
let changed = foo.push(4);
foo === changed // false
console.log(foo.toJS()); // [ 1, 2, 3 ]
console.log(changed.toJS()); // [ 1, 2, 3, 4 ]
```

In order to take advantage of immutability, we will need to install Immutable.js using npm.

The library is already a part of the project that contains the code for the book. You can find a reference to Immutable.js in `package.json`, located in the root of the project. You can take a look at `ch4/ts/change_detection_strategy/app.ts` to see how we include the immutable collections in our TypeScript application.

Now, it's time to refactor our to-do application and make it use immutable data.

Using immutable data in Angular

Let's take a look at how we currently keep the to-do items in the `TodoApp` component:

```
class TodoApp {
  todos: Todo[] = [...];
  ...
}
```

We use an array of `Todo` items. The JavaScript array is mutable, which means that if we pass it to a component that uses the `OnPush` strategy, it is not safe to skip the change detection in case we get the same input reference. For instance, we may have two components that use the same list of to-do items. Both components can modify the list since it is mutable. This will lead to an inconsistent state for any of the components in case their change detection is not performed. That's why we need to make sure that the list that holds the items is immutable. All we need to do in the `TodoApp` component in order to make sure that it holds its data in an immutable data structure is this:

```
// ch4/ts/change_detection_strategy/app.ts
class TodoApp {
  todos: Immutable.fromJS([{
    label: 'Buy milk',
    completed: false
  }, {
    label: 'Save the world',
    completed: false
  }]);
  ...
}
```

In this way, we construct the `todos` property as an immutable list, which contains immutable objects; all we need to do is to invoke the function `fromJS` exported by Immutable.js. It will recursively turn any JavaScript object into an immutable object.

Next, since the mutation operations of the immutable list return a new list, we need to make a slight modification in `addTodo` and `toggleTodoCompletion`:

```
...
addTodo(label: string) {
  this.todos = this.todos.push(Immutable.fromJS({
    label,
    completed: false
  }));
}

toggleCompletion(index: number) {
  this.todos = this.todos.update(index, todo => {
    return Immutable.fromJS({
      label: todo.label,
      completed: !todo.completed
    });
  });
}
...
```

The `addTodo` function looks exactly the same as before, except that we set the result of the `push` method as a value to the `todos` property.

In `toggleTodoCompletion`, we use the `update` method of the immutable list. As the first argument, we pass the index of the to-do item we want to modify, and the second argument is a callback that does the actual modification. Note that since we use immutable data in this case, we copy the modified to-do item. This is required because it tells the `update` method that the item with the given index has been changed (since it is immutable, it is considered as changed only when it has a new reference), which means that the entire list has been changed.

That was the complex part! Now, let's take a look at the `TodoList` component's definition:

```
@Component({
  selector: 'todo-list',
  changeDetection: ChangeDetectionStrategy.OnPush,
  template: `...`,
  styles: [...]
})
class TodoList {
  @Input() todos: ImmutableList<Todo>;
  @Output() toggle = new EventEmitter<number>();

  toggleCompletion(index: number) {
    this.toggle.emit(index);
  }
```

```
    }
```

Finally, we need to modify the way we access the properties of the immutable to-do items inside the templates:

```
<ul>
  <li *ngFor="let todo of todos; let index = index"
      [class.completed]="todo.get('completed')">
    <input type="checkbox" [checked]="todo.get('completed')"
      (change)="toggleCompletion(index)">
  {{todo.get('label')}}
  </li>
</ul>
```

The change we made here is that instead of using direct property access, such as `todo.completed`, we invoke the object's `get` method by passing the property the value we want to get as a string, in this case `"completed"`.

Inside the `@Component` decorator, we set the `changeDetection` property to the value of the `OnPush` strategy. This means that the component will run its change detector only when any of its inputs gets a new reference. Everything else, except the property access, inside of the template of the component stays exactly the same since `ngForOf` internally uses ES2015 iterators to loop over the items in the provided collection. They are supported by Immutable.js, so no changes in the template are required.

Since we need the index of the changed item instead of its reference (the one we use in the `update` method of the `todos` collection in `TodoApp`), we change the type of the output of the component to `EventEmitter<number>`. In `toggleCompletion`, we emit the index of the changed to-do item.

This is how we optimized our simple to-do application by preventing the change detection mechanism from running in the entire right subtree, in case the parent component hasn't pushed an input with a new reference.

Summary

In this chapter, we went through the core building blocks of an Angular application: directives and components. We built a couple of sample components, which showed us the syntax to be used for the definition of these fundamental concepts. We also described the life cycle of each directive and the core set of features the given directive and component have. As the next step, we saw how we can enhance the performance of our application using the `OnPush` change detection strategy with an immutable data.

The next chapter is completely dedicated to the Angular services and the dependency injection mechanism of the framework. We will take a look at how we can define and instantiate custom injectors and how we can take advantage of the dependency injection mechanism in our directives and components.

5
Dependency Injection in Angular

In this chapter, we'll explain how to take advantage of the **dependency injection** (**DI**) mechanism of the framework, with all its various features.

We will explore the following topics:

- Configuring and creating injectors.
- Instantiating objects using injectors.
- Injecting dependencies into directives and components–this way, we will be able to reuse the business logic defined within the services and wire it up with the UI logic.
- Annotating ES5 code in order to get the exact same result we get when we use the TypeScript syntax.

Why do I need DI?

Let's suppose that we have a `Car` class that depends on `Engine` and `Transmission` classes. How can we implement this system? Let's take a look:

```
class Engine {...}

class Transmission {...}

class Car {
  engine;
  transmission;
```

```
  constructor() {
    this.engine = new Engine();
    this.transmission = new Transmission();
  }
}
```

In the preceding example, we create the dependencies of the `Car` class inside its constructor. Although it looks simple, it is far from being flexible. Each time we create an instance of the `Car` class, in its constructor, instances of the same `Engine` and `Transmission` classes will be created. This may be problematic because of the following reasons:

- The `Car` class gets less testable because we can't test it independently of its `engine` and `transmission` dependencies.
- We couple the `Car` class with the logic used for the instantiation of its dependencies.

DI in Angular

Another way we can approach this is by taking advantage of the DI pattern. We're already familiar with it from AngularJS; let's demonstrate how we can refactor the preceding code using DI in the context of Angular:

```
class Engine {...}
class Transmission {...}

@Injectable()
class Car {
  engine;
  transmission;

  constructor(engine: Engine, transmission: Transmission) {
    this.engine = engine;
    this.transmission = transmission;
  }
}
```

All we did in the preceding snippet was add the `@Injectable` class decorator on top of the definition of the `Car` class and provide type annotations for the parameters of its constructor.

Benefits of DI

There is one more step left, which we'll take a look at in the next section. Before that, let's take a look at what the benefits of the mentioned approach are:

- We can easily pass different versions of the dependencies of the `Car` class for a testing environment, or for instantiating different `Car` models.
- We're not coupled with the logic around the dependencies' instantiation.

The `Car` class is only responsible for implementing its own domain-specific logic instead of being coupled with additional functionalities, such as the management of its dependencies. Our code also got more declarative and easier to read.

Now, that we've realized some of the benefits of DI, let's take a look at the missing pieces in order to make this code work.

Configuring an injector

The primitive used for the instantiation of the individual dependencies in our Angular applications via the DI mechanism of the framework is called the **injector**. The injector contains a set of **providers** that encapsulate the logic for the instantiation of registered dependencies associated with **tokens**. We can think of tokens as identifiers of the different providers registered within the injector.

Let's take a look at the following snippet, which is located at `ch5/ts/injector-basics/injector.ts`:

```
import 'reflect-metadata';
import {
  ReflectiveInjector,
  Inject,
  Injectable,
  OpaqueToken
} from '@angular/core';

const BUFFER_SIZE = new OpaqueToken('buffer-size');

class Buffer {
  constructor(@Inject(BUFFER_SIZE) private size: Number) {
    console.log(this.size);
  }
}
```

```
@Injectable()
class Socket {
  constructor(private buffer: Buffer) {}
}

let injector = ReflectiveInjector.resolveAndCreate([
  { provide: BUFFER_SIZE, useValue: 42 },
  Buffer,
  Socket
]);

injector.get(Socket);
```

You can run the file using the following command:

```
$ cd app
$ ts-node ch5/ts/injector-basics/injector.ts
```

If you haven't installed `ts-node` yet, take a look at Chapter 3, *TypeScript Crash Course*, which explains how you can proceed in order to have it up and running on your computer.

We then import `ReflectiveInjector`, `Injectable`, `Inject`, `OpaqueToken`, and `provide`.

Injector represents an abstract **container** used for the instantiation of the different dependencies; `ReflectiveInjector` is a concrete class, which implements this abstraction. Using rules like the one declared, with the object literal passed as first argument to `resolveAndCreate` and the metadata generated by the TypeScript compiler, `ReflectiveInjector` knows how to create the different dependencies.

In the preceding snippet, we initially define the `BUFFER_SIZE` constant and set it to the `new OpaqueToken('buffer-size')` value. We can think of the value of `BUFFER_SIZE` as a unique value that cannot be duplicated in the application (`OpaqueToken` is an alternative of the `Symbol` class from ES2015, since at the time of writing this book, it is not supported by TypeScript).

We defined two classes: `Buffer` and `Socket`. The `Buffer` class has a constructor that accepts only a single dependency called `size`, which is of the type `Number`. In order to add additional metadata for the process of dependency resolution, we use the `@Inject` parameter decorator. This decorator accepts an identifier (also known as **token**) for the dependency we want to inject. Usually, it is the type of the dependency (that is, a reference of a class), but in some cases, it can be a different type of value. For example, in our case, we used the instance of the `OpaqueToken` class.

Dependency resolution with generated metadata

Now, let's take a look at the `Socket` class. We decorate it with the `@Injectable` decorator. This decorator is supposed to be used by any class that accepts dependencies that should be injected via the DI mechanism of Angular.

The `@Injectable` decorator forces the TypeScript compiler to generate additional metadata for the types of dependencies that a given class accepts. This means that, if we omit the `@Injectable` decorator, Angular's DI mechanism will not be aware of the tokens associated with the dependencies it needs to resolve.

TypeScript doesn't generate any metadata if no decorator is used on top of a class, mostly for performance concerns. Imagine, if such metadata was generated for each individual class that accepts dependencies–in this case, the output would be bloated with an additional type metadata that would be unused.

An alternative to using `@Injectable` is to explicitly declare the tokens of the dependencies using the `@Inject` decorator. Take a look at the following:

```
class Socket {
  constructor(@Inject(Buffer) private buffer: Buffer) {}
}
```

This means that the preceding code has equivalent semantics to the code that uses `@Injectable`, as mentioned earlier. The only difference is that Angular will get the type of dependency (that is, the token associated with it) explicitly (directly from the metadata added by the `@Inject` decorator) as compared to the case where `@Injectable` is used, when it will look at the metadata generated by the compiler.

Instantiating an injector

Now, let's create an instance of an injector in order to use it for the instantiation of registered tokens:

```
let injector = ReflectiveInjector.resolveAndCreate([
  { provide: BUFFER_SIZE, useValue: 42 },
  Buffer,
  Socket
]);
```

We create an instance of the `ReflectiveInjector` using its static method called `resolveAndCreate`. This is a factory method that accepts an array of providers as argument and returns a new `ReflectiveInjector`.

`resolve` means that the providers will go through a resolution process, which includes some internal processing (flattening multiple nested arrays and converting individual providers into an array). Later, the injector can instantiate any of the dependencies for which we have registered providers based on the rules the providers encapsulate.

In our case, with the provider's declaration we explicitly tell the Angular's DI mechanism to use the value `42` when the `BUFFER_SIZE` token is required. The other two providers are implicit. Angular will instantiate them by invoking the provided class with the `new` operator once all of their dependencies are resolved.

We request the `BUFFER_SIZE` value in the constructor of the `Buffer` class:

```
class Buffer {
  constructor(@Inject(BUFFER_SIZE) private size: Number) {
    console.log(this.size);
  }
}
```

In the preceding example, we use the `@Inject` parameter decorator. It hints the DI mechanism that the first argument of the constructor of the `Buffer` class should be instantiated with the provider associated with the `BUFFER_SIZE` token passed to the injector.

Introducing forward references

Angular introduced the concept of **forward references**. It is required due to the following reasons:

- ES2015 classes are not hoisted.
- Allowing resolution of the dependencies that are declared after the declaration of the dependent providers.

In this section, we will explain the problem that forward references solve and the way we can take advantage of them.

Now, let's suppose that we have defined the `Buffer` and `Socket` classes in the opposite order:

```
// ch5/ts/injector-basics/forward-ref.ts

@Injectable()
class Socket {
  constructor(private buffer: Buffer) {...}
```

```
}

// undefined
console.log(Buffer);

class Buffer {
  constructor(@Inject(BUFFER_SIZE) private size: Number) {...}
}

// [Function: Buffer]
console.log(Buffer);
```

Here, we have the exact same dependencies as the ones in the previous example but, in this case, the `Socket` class definition precedes the definition of the `Buffer` class. Note that the value of the `Buffer` identifier will equal `undefined` until the JavaScript virtual machine evaluates the declaration of the `Buffer` class. However, the metadata for the types of dependencies that `Socket` accepts will be generated and placed right after the `Socket` class definition. This means that, during the interpretation of the generated JavaScript, the value of the `Buffer` identifier will equal `undefined`–that is, as a type of dependency (or in the context of the DI mechanism of Angular, its token), the framework will get an invalid value.

Running the preceding snippet will result in a runtime error of the following form:

Error: Cannot resolve all parameters for Socket(undefined). Make sure they all have valid type or annotations.

The best way to resolve this issue is by swapping the definitions with their proper order. Another way we can proceed is to take advantage of a solution that Angular provides–a forward reference:

```
...
import {forwardRef} from '@angular/core';
...

@Injectable()
class Socket {
  constructor(@Inject(forwardRef(() => Buffer))
    private buffer: Buffer) {}
}

class Buffer {...}
```

The preceding snippet demonstrates how we can take advantage of forward references. All we need to do is invoke the @Inject parameter decorator with argument the result of the invocation of the forwardRef function. The forwardRef function is a higher-order function that accepts a single argument–another function that is responsible for returning the token associated with the dependency (or more precisely associated with its provider) that needs to be injected. This way, the framework provides a way to defer the process of resolving the types (tokens) of dependencies.

The token of the dependency will be resolved the first time Socket needs to be instantiated, unlike the default behavior in which the token is required at the time of the declaration of the given class.

Configuring providers

Now, let's take a look at an example similar to the one used earlier, but with a different configuration of the injector:

```
let injector = ReflectiveInjector.resolveAndCreate([
  { provide: BUFFER_SIZE, useValue: 42 },
  { provide: Buffer, useClass: Buffer },
  { provide: Socket, useClass: Socket }
]);
```

In this case, inside the provider, we explicitly declared that we want the Buffer class to be used for the construction of the dependency with a token equal to the reference of the Buffer class. We do the exact same thing for the dependency associated with the Socket token; but, this time, we provided the Socket class instead. This is how Angular will proceed when we omit the explicit provider declaration and pass only a reference to a class instead.

Explicitly declaring the class used for the creation of an instance of the same class may seem quite worthless, and given the examples we have looked at so far, that'd be completely correct. In some cases, however, we might want to provide a different class for the instantiation of a dependency associated with a given class token.

For example, let's suppose we have the Http service that is used in a service called UserService:

```
class Http {...}

@Injectable()
class UserService {
  constructor(private http: Http) {}
```

```
}

let injector = ReflectiveInjector.resolveAndCreate([
  UserService,
  Http
]);
```

The `UserService` service uses `Http` for communication with a RESTful service. We can instantiate `UserService` using `injector.get(UserService)`. This way, the constructor of `UserService` invoked by the injector's `get` method will accept an instance of the `Http` service as an argument. However, if we want to test `UserService`, we don't really need to make HTTP calls to the RESTful service. In the case of unit testing, we can provide a dummy implementation that will only fake these HTTP calls. In order to inject an instance of a different class to the `UserService` service, we can change the configuration of the injector to the following:

```
class DummyHttp {...}

// ...

let injector = ReflectiveInjector.resolveAndCreate([
  UserService,
  { provide: Http, useClass: DummyHttp }
]);
```

Now, when we instantiate `UserService`, its constructor will receive a reference to an instance of the `DummyHttp` service. This code is available at `ch5/ts/configuring-providers/dummy-http.ts`.

Using existing providers

Another way to proceed is by using the `useExisting` property of the provider's configuration object:

```
// ch5/ts/configuring-providers/existing.ts
let injector = ReflectiveInjector.resolveAndCreate([
  DummyService,
  { provide: Http, useExisting: DummyService },
  UserService
]);
```

In the preceding snippet, we register three tokens: `DummyService`, `UserService`, and `Http`. We declare that we want to bind the `Http` token to the existing token, `DummyService`. This means that, when the `Http` service is requested, the injector will find the provider for the token used as the value of the `useExisting` property and instantiate it or get the value associated with it. We can think of `useExisting` as creating an alias of the given token:

```
let dummyHttp = {
  get() {},
  post() {}
};
let injector = ReflectiveInjector.resolveAndCreate([
  { provide: DummyService, useValue: dummyHttp },
  { provide: Http, useExisting: DummyService },
  UserService
]);
console.assert(injector.get(UserService).http === dummyHttp);
```

The preceding snippet will create an alias of the `Http` token to the `DummyHttp` token. This means that once the `Http` token is requested, the call will be forwarded to the provider associated with the `DummyHttp` token, which will be resolved to the value of `dummyHttp`.

Defining factories for instantiating services

Now, let's suppose that we want to create a complex object, for example, one that represents a **Transport Layer Security** (**TLS**) connection. A few of the properties of such an object are a socket, a set of crypto protocols, and a certificate. In the context of this problem, the features of the DI mechanism of Angular we have looked at so far might seem a bit limited.

For example, we might need to configure some of the properties of the `TLSConnection` class without coupling the process of its instantiation with all the configuration details (choose appropriate crypto algorithms, open the TCP socket over which we will establish the secure connection, and so on).

In this case, we can take advantage of the `useFactory` property of the provider's configuration object:

```
let injector = ReflectiveInjector.resolveAndCreate([
  {
    provide: TLSConnection,
    useFactory: (socket: Socket, certificate: Certificate, crypto: Crypto)
      => {
        let connection = new TLSConnection();
```

```
            connection.certificate = certificate;
            connection.socket = socket;
            connection.crypto = crypto;
            socket.open();
            return connection;
        },
        deps: [Socket, Certificate, Crypto]
    },
    { BUFFER_SIZE, useValue: 42 },
    Buffer,
    Socket,
    Certificate,
    Crypto
]);
```

The snippet above seems a bit complex at first, but let's take a look at it step-by-step. We can start with the parts we're already familiar with:

```
let injector = ReflectiveInjector.resolveAndCreate([
    ...
    { BUFFER_SIZE, useValue: 42 },
    Buffer,
    Socket,
    Certificate,
    Crypto
]);
```

Initially, we register a number of providers: `Buffer`, `Socket`, `Certificate`, and `Crypto`. Just like in the preceding example, we also register the `BUFFER_SIZE` token and associated it with the value `42`. This means that we can already create objects of the `Buffer`, `Socket`, `Certificate`, and `Crypto` types, as follows:

```
// buffer with size 42
console.log(injector.get(Buffer));
// socket with buffer with size 42
console.log(injector.get(Socket));
```

We can create and configure an instance of the `TLSConnection` object in the following way:

```
let connection = new TLSConnection();
connection.certificate = certificate;
connection.socket = socket;
connection.crypto = crypto;
socket.open();
return connection;
```

Now, if we register a provider that has the `TLSConnection` token as a dependency, we will prevent the DI mechanism of Angular from taking care of the dependency resolution process. In order to handle this problem, we can use the `useFactory` property of the provider's configuration object. This way, we can specify a function in which we can manually create the instance of the object associated with the provider's token. We can use the `useFactory` property together with the `deps` property in order to specify the dependencies to be passed to the factory:

```
{
  provide: TLSConnection,
  useFactory: (socket: Socket, certificate: Certificate, crypto: Crypto) =>
  {
    // ...
  },
  deps: [Socket, Certificate, Crypto]
}
```

In the preceding snippet, we define the factory function used for the instantiation of `TLSConnection`. As dependencies, we declare `Socket`, `Certificate`, and `Crypto`. These dependencies are resolved by the DI mechanism of Angular and injected into the factory function. You can take a look at the entire implementation and play with it at `ch5/ts/configuring-providers/factory.ts`.

Child injectors and visibility

In this section, we will take a look at how we can build a hierarchy of injectors. This is a completely new concept in the framework introduced by Angular 2. Each injector can have either zero or one parent injectors, and each parent injector can have zero or more children. In contrast to AngularJS where all the registered providers are stored in a flat structure, in Angular 2 and later versions, they are stored in a tree. The flat structure is more limited; for instance, it doesn't support the namespacing of tokens; we cannot declare different providers for the same token, which might be required in some cases. So far, we have looked at an example of an injector that doesn't have any children or a parent. Now, let's build a hierarchy of injectors.

In order to gain a better understanding of this hierarchical structure of injectors, let's take a look at the following diagram:

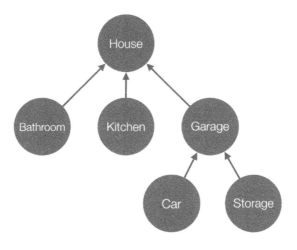

Figure 1

Here, we see a tree where each node is an injector, and each of these injectors keeps a reference to its parent. The injector **House** has three child injectors: **Bathroom**, **Kitchen**, and **Garage**.

Garage has two child injectors: **Car** and **Storage**. We can think of these injectors as containers with registered providers inside of them.

Let's suppose that we want to get the value of the provider associated with the token **Tire**. If we use the injector **Car**, this means that Angular's DI mechanism will try to find the provider associated with this token in **Car** and all of its parents, **Garage** and **House**, until it finds it.

Building a hierarchy of injectors

In order to gain a better understanding of the paragraph, let's take a look at this simple example:

```
// ch5/ts/parent-child/simple-example.ts

class Http {}

@Injectable()
class UserService {
  constructor(public http: Http) {}
}

let parentInjector = ReflectiveInjector.resolveAndCreate([
```

```
  Http
]);

let childInjector = parentInjector.resolveAndCreateChild([
  UserService
]);

// UserService { http: Http {} }
console.log(childInjector.get(UserService));
// true
console.log(childInjector.get(Http) === parentInjector.get(Http));
```

The imports are omitted since they are not essential to explain the code. We have two services, Http and UserService, where UserService depends on the Http service.

Initially, we create an injector using the resolveAndCreate static method of the ReflectiveInjector class. We pass an implicit provider to this injector, which will later be resolved to a provider with an Http token. Using resolveAndCreateChild, we resolve the passed providers and instantiate an injector, which points to parentInjector (so, we get the same relation as the one between **Garage** and **House** shown in the previous diagram).

Now, using childInjector.get(UserService), we are able to get the value associated with the UserService token. Similarly, using childInjector.get(Http) and parentInjector.get(Http), we get the same value associated with the Http token. This means that childInjector asks its parent for the value associated with the requested token.

However, if we try to use parentInjector.get(UserService), we won't be able to get the value associated with the token, since its provider is registered in childInjector.

Configuring dependencies

Now that we're familiar with the injectors' hierarchy, let's see how we can get the dependencies from the appropriate injectors in it.

Using the @Self decorator

Now, let's suppose that we have the following configuration:

```
abstract class Channel {}
```

```
class Http extends Channel {}

class WebSocket extends Channel {}

@Injectable()
class UserService {
  constructor(public channel: Channel) {}
}

let parentInjector = ReflectiveInjector.resolveAndCreate([
  { provide: Channel, useClass: Http }
]);

let childInjector = parentInjector.resolveAndCreateChild([
  { provide: Channel, useClass: WebSocket },
  UserService
]);
```

We can instantiate the UserService token using:

```
childInjector.get(UserService);
```

In UserService, we can declare that we want to get the Channel dependency from the current injector (that is, childInjector) using the @Self decorator:

```
@Injectable()
class UserService {
  constructor(@Self() public channel: Channel) {}
}
```

Although this will be the default behavior during the instantiation of the UserService, using @Self, we can be more explicit. Let's suppose that we change the configuration of childInjector to the following:

```
let parentInjector = ReflectiveInjector.resolveAndCreate([
  { provide: Channel, useClass: Http }
]);

let childInjector = parentInjector.resolveAndCreateChild([
  UserService
]);
```

If we keep the @Self decorator in the UserService constructor and try to instantiate UserService using childInjector, we will get a runtime error because of the missing provider for Channel.

Skipping the self injector

In some cases, we may want to use the provider registered in the parent injector instead of the one registered in the current injector. We can achieve this behavior by taking advantage of the `@SkipSelf` decorator. For instance, let's suppose that we have the following definition of the `Context` class:

```
class Context {
  constructor(public parentContext: Context) {}
}
```

Each instance of the `Context` class has a parent. Now, let's build a hierarchy of two injectors, which will allow us to create a context with a parent context:

```
let parentInjector = ReflectiveInjector.resolveAndCreate([
  { provide: Context, useValue: new Context(null) }
]);

let childInjector = parentInjector.resolveAndCreateChild([
  Context
]);
```

Since the root context doesn't have a parent, we will set the value of its provider to be `new Context(null)`.

If we want to instantiate the child context, we can use:

```
childInjector.get(Context);
```

For the instantiation of the child, `Context` will be used by the provider registered within the `childInjector`. However, as a dependency, it accepts an object that is an instance of the `Context` class. Such classes exist in the same injector, which means that Angular will try to instantiate it, but it has a dependency of the `Context` type. This process will lead to an infinite loop that will cause a runtime error.

In order to prevent it from happening, we can change the definition of `Context` in the following way:

```
class Context {
  constructor(@SkipSelf() public parentContext: Context) {}
}
```

The only change that we introduced is the addition of the parameter decorator `@SkipSelf`.

Having optional dependencies

Angular 2 introduced the `@Optional` decorator, which allows us to deal with dependencies that don't have a registered provider associated with them. Let's suppose that a dependency of a provider is not available in any of the target injectors responsible for its instantiation. If we use the `@Optional` decorator, during the instantiation of the dependent provider the value of the missing dependency will be passed `null`.

Now, let's take a look at the following example:

```
abstract class SortingAlgorithm {
  abstract sort(collection: BaseCollection): BaseCollection;
}

@Injectable()
class Collection extends BaseCollection {
  private sort: SortingAlgorithm;

  constructor(sort: SortingAlgorithm) {
    super();
    this.sort = sort || this.getDefaultSort();
  }
}

let injector = ReflectiveInjector.resolveAndCreate([
  Collection
]);
```

In this case, we defined an abstract class called `SortingAlgorithm` and a class called `Collection`, which accepts an instance of a concrete class as a dependency that extends `SortingAlgorithm`. Inside the `Collection` constructor, we set the `sort` instance property to the passed dependency of the `SortingAlgorithm` type or a default sorting algorithm implementation.

We didn't define any providers for the `SortingAlgorithm` token in the injector we configured. So, if we want to get an instance of the `Collection` class using `injector.get(Collection)`, we'll get a runtime error. This means that if we want to get an instance of the `Collection` class using the DI mechanism of the framework, we must register a provider for the `SortingAlgorithm` token, although we may want to fall back to a default sorting algorithm, returned by the `getDefaultSort` method.

Angular provides a solution to this problem with the `@Optional` decorator. This is how we can approach the problem using it:

```
// ch5/ts/decorators/optional.ts
```

```
@Injectable()
class Collection extends BaseCollection {
  private sort: SortingAlgorithm;

  constructor(@Optional() sort: SortingAlgorithm) {
    super();
    this.sort = sort || this.getDefaultSort();
  }
}
```

In the preceding snippet, we declare the `sort` dependency as optional, which means that if Angular doesn't find any provider for its token, it will pass the `null` value.

Using multiproviders

Multiproviders are another new concept introduced to the DI mechanism of Angular in version 2. They allow us to associate multiple providers with the same token. This can be quite useful if we're developing a third-party library that comes with some default implementations of different services, but you want to allow the users to extend it with custom ones. They are also exclusively used to declare multiple validations over a single control in the Angular's form module. We will explain this module in Chapter 6, *Working with the Angular Router and Forms*, and Chapter 7, *Explaining Pipes and Communicating with RESTful Services*.

Another sample of an applicable use case of multiproviders is what Angular uses for event management in its Web Workers implementation. They create multiproviders for event management plugins. Each of the providers return a different strategy, which supports a different set of events (touch events, keyboard events, and so on). Once a given event occurs, they can choose the appropriate plugin that handles it.

Let's take a look at an example that illustrates a typical usage of multiproviders:

```
// ch5/ts/configuring-providers/multi-providers.ts
const VALIDATOR = new OpaqueToken('validator');

interface EmployeeValidator {
  (person: Employee): string;
}

class Employee {...}

let injector = ReflectiveInjector.resolveAndCreate([
  {
    provide: VALIDATOR,
    multi: true,
```

```
      useValue: (person: Employee) => {
        if (!person.name) {
          return 'The name is required';
        }
      }
    },
    {
      provide: VALIDATOR,
      multi: true,
      useValue: (person: Employee) => {
        if (!person.name || person.name.length < 1) {
          return 'The name should be more than 1 symbol long';
        }
      }
    },
    Employee
]);
```

In the preceding snippet, we declare a constant called VALIDATOR and as its value we set a new instance of OpaqueToken. We also create an injector where we register three providers–two of them provide functions that, based on different criteria, validate instances of the class Employee. These functions are of the type EmployeeValidator.

In order to declare that we want the injector to pass all the registered validators to the constructor of the Employee class, we need to use the following constructor definition:

```
class Employee {
  name: string;

  constructor(@Inject(VALIDATOR) private validators: EmployeeValidator[])
{}

  validate() {
    return this.validators
      .map(v => v(this))
      .filter(value => !!value);
  }
}
```

In the example, we declare a class Employee that accepts a single dependency: an array of EmployeeValidators. In the method validate, we apply the individual validators over the current class instance and filter the results in order to get only the ones that have returned an error message.

Note that the constructor argument validators is of the EmployeeValidator[] type. Since we can't use the type "array of objects" as a token for a provider, because it is not a valid value in JavaScript and can't be used as a token, we will need to use the `@Inject` parameter decorator.

Using DI with components and directives

In `Chapter 4`, *Getting Started with Angular Components and Directives*, when we developed our first Angular directive, we saw how we can take advantage of the DI mechanism to inject services into our UI-related components (that is, directives and components).

Let's take a quick look at what we did earlier, but from a DI perspective:

```
// ch4/ts/tooltip/app.ts

// ...
@Directive(...)
export class Tooltip {
  @Input() saTooltip: string;

  constructor(private el: ElementRef, private overlay: Overlay) {
    this.overlay.attach(el.nativeElement);
  }
  // ...
}

@Component({
  // ...
  providers: [Overlay]
})
class App {}
```

Most of the code from the earlier implementation is omitted because it is not directly related to our current focus.

Note that the constructor of `Tooltip` accepts two dependencies:

- An instance of the `ElementRef` class.
- An instance of the `Overlay` class.

The types of dependencies are the tokens associated with their providers and the corresponding values obtained from the providers will be injected with the DI mechanism of Angular.

Although the declaration of the dependencies of the `Tooltip` class looks exactly the same as what we did in the previous sections, there's neither any explicit configuration nor any instantiation of an injector. In this case, Angular internally creates and configures the so called **element injector**. We'll explain it a little bit later, but before that, lets take a look at how we can configure the DI mechanism using NgModules.

Configuring DI with NgModules

We have already talked about NgModules in `Chapter 2`, *The Building Blocks of an Angular Application* and `Chapter 4`, *Getting Started with Angular Components and Directives*. We mentioned that they help us to divide our application into logical parts; we also discussed how to use NgModules' imports and exports. In this section, we'll look at a brief overview of how we can use them to configure the providers of our application.

Based on the providers declared in a given NgModule, Angular will instantiate an injector. This injector will manage all the providers that are listed in the `providers` property of the object literal we pass to the `@NgModule` decorator:

```
class Markdown {...}

@Component(...)
class MarkdownPanel {...}

@Component(...)
class App {...}

@NgModule({
  declarations: [App, MarkdownPanel],
  providers: [Markdown],
  imports: [BrowserModule],
  bootstrap: [App],
})
class AppModule {}

platformBrowserDynamic().bootstrapModule(AppModule);
```

In the preceding example, we declare a single provider for the `Markdown` service. It will be available in all the components and directives listed in the `declarations` array because the injectors used by the top-level components will get the one configured through the NgModule as their parent injector.

Now, let's suppose that our module imports another module that has a declaration of providers:

```
// ch4/ts/directives-ngmodules/app.ts
// ...
```

```
@NgModule({
  declarations: [Button],
  exports: [Button],
  providers: [Markdown],
})
class ButtonModule {}

//...

@NgModule({
  declarations: [App, MarkdownPanel],
  imports: [BrowserModule, ButtonModule],
  bootstrap: [App],
})
class AppModule {}

platformBrowserDynamic().bootstrapModule(AppModule);
```

In the example, we have two modules — the `AppModule` we previously saw and `ButtonModule`. In the snippet `AppModule` imports `ButtonModule`, which means that all the exports of `ButtonModule` will be available as declarations in `AppModule`. On top of that, the providers declared in `ButtonModule` will be merged with the providers of `AppModule`. Based on all these providers, Angular will instantiate an injector and set it as a parent injector to the injector used by the bootstrap component – `App`.

Now, let's discuss the element injector that each component and directive has associated to it.

Introducing the element injectors

Under the hood, Angular will create injectors for all the directives and components, and add a default set of providers to them. These are the so-called **element injectors** and are something the framework takes care of itself. The injectors associated with the components are called **host injectors**. One of the providers in each element injector is associated with the `ElementRef` token; it will return a reference to the host element of the directive. However, where is the provider for the `Overlay` class declared? Let's take a look at the implementation of the top-level component:

```
@Component({
  // ...
  providers: [Overlay]
})
class App {}
```

We configure the element injector for the App component by declaring the providers property inside the @Component decorator. At this point, the registered providers will be visible by the directive or the component associated with the corresponding element injector and the component's entire component subtree, unless they are overridden somewhere in the hierarchy.

Declaring providers for the element injectors

Having the declaration of all the providers in the same place might be quite inconvenient. For example, imagine we're developing a large-scale application that has hundreds of components depending on thousands of services. In this case, configuring all the providers in the root component is not a practical solution. There will be name collisions when two or more providers are associated with the same token. The configuration will be huge, and it will be hard to trace where the different dependencies need to be injected.

As we mentioned, Angular's @Directive (and @Component) decorator allows us to introduce directive-specific providers using the providers property. Here is how we can approach this:

```
@Directive({
  selector: '[saTooltip]',
  providers: [{ provide: Overlay, useClass: OverlayMock }]
})
export class Tooltip {
 @Input() saTooltip: string;

  constructor(private el: ElementRef, private overlay: Overlay) {
    this.overlay.attach(el.nativeElement);
  }
  // ...
}

// ...

platformBrowserDynamic().bootstrapModule(AppModule);
```

The preceding example overrides the provider for the Overlay token in the Tooltip directive's declaration. This way, Angular will inject an instance of OverlayMock instead of Overlay during the instantiation of the tooltip.

Exploring DI with components

Since components are generally directives with views, everything we've seen so far regarding how the DI mechanism works with directives is valid for components as well. However, because of the extra features that the components provide, we're allowed to have further control over their providers.

As we said, the injector associated with each component will be marked as a **host** injector. There's a parameter decorator called @Host, which allows us to retrieve a given dependency from any injector until it reaches the closest host injector. This means that, using the @Host decorator in a directive, we can declare that we want to retrieve the given dependency from the current injector or any parent injector until we reach the injector of the closest parent component.

The viewProviders property added to the @Component decorator is in charge of achieving even more control.

viewProviders versus providers

Let's take a look at an example of a component called MarkdownPanel. This component will be used in the following way:

```
<markdown-panel>
  <panel-title># Title</pane-title>
  <panel-content>
# Content of the panel
* First point
* Second point
  </panel-content>
</markdown-panel>
```

The content of each section of the panel will be translated from markdown to HTML. We can delegate this functionality to a service called Markdown:

```
import * as markdown from 'markdown';

class Markdown {
  toHTML(md) {
    return markdown.toHTML(md);
  }
}
```

The Markdown service wraps the markdown module in order to make it injectable through the DI mechanism.

Now let's implement `MarkdownPanel`.

In the following snippet, we can find all the important details from the component's implementation:

```
// ch5/ts/directives/app.ts
@Component({
  selector: 'markdown-panel',
  viewProviders: [Markdown],
  styles: [...],
  template: `
    <div class="panel">
      <div class="panel-title">
        <ng-content select="panel-title"></ng-content>
      </div>
      <div class="panel-content">
        <ng-content select="panel-content"></ng-content>
      </div>
    </div>`
})
class MarkdownPanel {
  constructor(private el: ElementRef, private md: Markdown) {}

  ngAfterContentInit() {
    let el = this.el.nativeElement;
    let title = el.querySelector('panel-title');
    let content = el.querySelector('panel-content');
    title.innerHTML = this.md.toHTML(title.innerHTML);
    content.innerHTML = this.md.toHTML(content.innerHTML);
  }
}
```

In the `@Component` decorator, we use the `markdown-panel` selector and set the `viewProviders` property. In this case, there's only a single view provider: the one for the `Markdown` service. By setting this property, we declare that all the providers declared in it will be accessible from the component itself and all of its **view children**.

Now, let's suppose we have a component called `MarkdownButton` and we want to add it to our template in the following way:

```
<markdown-panel>
  <panel-title>### Small title</panel-title>
  <panel-content>
    Some code
  </panel-content>
  <markdown-button>*Click to toggle*</markdown-button>
</markdown-panel>
```

The `Markdown` service will not be accessible by the `MarkdownButton` used below the `panel-content` element; however, it'll be accessible if we use the button in the component's template:

```
@Component({
  selector: 'markdown-panel',
  viewProviders: [Markdown],
  styles: [...],
  template: `
    <div class="panel">
      <markdown-button>*Click to toggle*</markdown-button>
      <div class="panel-title">
        <ng-content select="panel-title"></ng-content>
      </div>
      <div class="panel-content">
        <ng-content select="panel-content"></ng-content>
      </div>
    </div>`
})
```

If we need the provider to be visible in all the content and view children, all we should do is change the name of the property `viewProviders` to `providers`.

You can find this example in the examples directory at `ch5/ts/directives/app.ts`.

 Note that, for any component or directive, we can override an existing provider declared in a NgModule using the `providers` properties of the object literal we pass to the `@Component` or the `@Directive` decorators. If we want to override a specific provider only for the view children of a given component, we can use `viewProviders`.

Using Angular's DI with ES5

We are already proficient in using the DI of Angular with TypeScript! As we know, we are not limited to TypeScript for the development of Angular applications; we can also use ES5, ES2015, and ES2016 (as well as Dart, but that is outside the scope of this book).

So far, we declared the dependencies of the different classes in their constructor using standard TypeScript type annotations. All such classes are supposed to be decorated with the `@Injectable` decorator. Unfortunately, some of the other languages supported by Angular miss a few of these features. In the following table, we can see that ES5 doesn't support type annotations, classes, and decorators:

	ES5	ES2015	ES2016
Classes	No	Yes	Yes
Decorators	No	No	Yes (no parameter decorators)
Type annotations	No	No	No

How can we take advantage of the DI mechanism in these languages? Angular provides an internal JavaScript **domain-specific language (DSL)**, which allows us to take advantage of the entire functionalities of the framework using ES5.

Now, let's translate the `MarkdownPanel` example we took a look at in the previous section from TypeScript to ES5. First, let's start with the `Markdown` service:

```
// ch5/es5/simple-example/app.js

var Markdown = ng.core.Class({
  constructor: function () {},
  toHTML: function (md) {
    return markdown.toHTML(md);
  }
});
```

We defined a variable called `Markdown` and set its value to the returned result from the invocation of `ng.core.Class`. This construct allows us to emulate ES2015 classes using ES5. The argument of the `ng.core.Class` method is an object literal, which must have the definition of a `constructor` function. As a result, `ng.core.Class` will return a JavaScript constructor function with the body of `constructor` from the object literal. All the other methods defined within the boundaries of the passed parameter will be added to the function's prototype.

One problem is solved: we can now emulate classes in ES5; there are two more problems left!

Now, let's take a look at how we can define the `MarkdownPanel` component:

```
// ch5/es5/simple-example/app.js

var MarkdownPanel = ng.core.Component({
  selector: 'markdown-panel',
  viewProviders: [Markdown],
  styles: [...],
  template: '...'
})
```

```
.Class({
  constructor: [Markdown, ng.core.ElementRef, function (md, el) {
    this.md = md;
    this.el = el;
  }],
  ngAfterContentInit: function () {
    ...
  }
});
```

From Chapter 4, *Getting Started with Angular Components and Directives*, we are already familiar with the ES5 syntax used to define components. Now, let's take a look at the constructor function of MarkdownPanel, in order to check how we can declare the dependencies of our components and classes in general.

From the preceding snippet, we should notice that the value of the constructor is not a function this time, but an array instead. This might seem familiar to you from AngularJS, where we are able to declare the dependencies of the given service by listing their names:

```
Module.service('UserMapper',
  ['User', '$http', function (User, $http) {
    // ...
  }]);
```

Although the new syntax looks similar, it brings some improvements. For instance, we're no longer limited to using strings for the dependencies' tokens.

Now, let's suppose we want to make the Markdown service an optional dependency. In this case, we can approach this by passing an array of decorators:

```
...
.Class({
  constructor: [[ng.core.Optional(), Markdown],
    ng.core.ElementRef, function (md, el) {
      this.md = md;
      this.el = el;
    }],
  ngAfterContentInit: function () {
    ...
  }
});
...
```

This way, by nesting arrays, we can apply a sequence of decorators:
`[[ng.core.Optional(), ng.core.Self(), Markdown], ...]`. In this example, the
`@Optional` and `@Self` decorators will add the associated metadata to the class in the
specified order.

 Although using ES5 makes our build simpler and allows us to skip the
intermediate step of transpilation, which can be tempting, Google's
recommendation is to take advantage of static typing using TypeScript.
This way, we have a much clearer syntax, which carries better semantics
with less typing and provides us with great tooling, including the
straightforward process of AoT compilation (we'll explore the Angular's
AoT in the final chapter of the book).

Summary

In this chapter, we covered the DI mechanism of Angular. We briefly discussed the
positives of using DI in our projects by introducing it in the context of the framework. The
second step in our journey was how to instantiate and configure injectors; we also explained
the injectors' hierarchy and the visibility of the registered providers. In order to enforce a
better separation of concerns, we mentioned how we can inject services carrying the
business logic of our application in our directives and components. The last point we took a
look at was how we can use the DI mechanism with the ES5 syntax.

In the next chapter, we'll introduce the new routing mechanism of the framework. We'll
explain how we can configure the component-based router and add multiple views to our
application. Another important topic we will cover is the new form module. By building a
simple application, we will demonstrate how we can create and manage forms.

6
Working with the Angular Router and Forms

By now, we're already familiar with the core of the framework. We know how to define components and directives in order to develop the view of our applications. We also know how to encapsulate business-related logic into services and wire everything together with the DI mechanism of Angular.

In this chapter, we'll explain a few more concepts that will help us build real-life Angular applications. They are as follows:

- The component-based router of the framework.
- Using Angular's forms module.
- Developing custom form validators.
- Developing template-driven forms.

Let's begin!

Developing the "Coders repository" application

Throughout the process of explaining the listed concepts, we'll develop a sample application that contains a repository of developers. Before we start coding, let's discuss the structure of the application.

The "Coders repository" will allow its users to add developers, either by filling a form with details about them, or by providing the GitHub handle for the developer and importing their profile from GitHub.

 For the purpose of this chapter, we will store information about the developers in memory, which means that, after the page is refreshed, we'll lose all the data stored during the session.

The application will have the following views:

- A list of all the developers.
- A view for adding or importing new developers.
- A view that shows the given developer's details. This view has two subviews:
    - **Basic details**: Shows the name of the developer and their GitHub avatar if available.
    - **Advanced profile**: Shows all the details known of the developer.

The end result of the application's home page will look as follows:

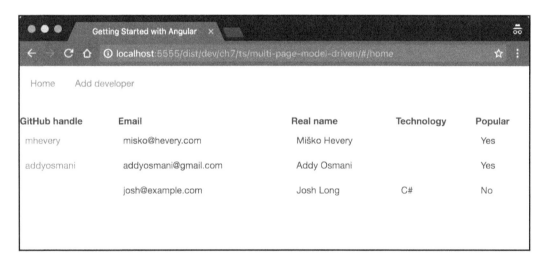

Figure 1

 In this chapter, we will build only a few of the listed views. The rest of the application will be explained in `Chapter 7`, *Explaining Pipes and Communicating with RESTful Services*.

Each developer will be an instance of the following class:

```
// ch6/ts/multi-page-template-driven/developer.ts

export class Developer {
  public id: number;
  public githubHandle: string;
  public avatarUrl: string;
  public realName: string;
  public email: string;
  public technology: string;
  public popular: boolean;
}
```

All the developers will reside within the DeveloperCollection class:

```
// ch6/ts/multi-page-template-driven/developer_collection.ts

class DeveloperCollection {
  private developers: Developer[] = [];

  getUserByGitHubHandle(username: string) {
    return this.developers
            .filter(u => u.githubHandle === username)
            .pop();
  }

  getUserById(id: number) {
    return this.developers
            .filter(u => u.id === id)
            .pop();
  }

  addDeveloper(dev: Developer) {
    this.developers.push(dev);
  }

  getAll() {
    return this.developers;
  }
}
```

The classes mentioned here encapsulate a simple business logic and don't have anything Angular-specific, so we won't get into any details.

Now, let's continue with the implementation by exploring the new router.

Exploring the Angular router

As we already know, in order to bootstrap any Angular application, we need to develop a root NgModule and a bootstrap component. The "Coders repository" application is not any different; the only addition in this specific case is that we will have multiple pages that need to be connected together with the Angular router.

Let's start with the imports required for the router's configuration and define the root component right after this:

```
// ch6/ts/step-0/app.ts

import {
  APP_BASE_HREF,
  LocationStrategy,
  HashLocationStrategy
} from '@angular/common';

import {RouterModule} from '@angular/router';
```

In the preceding snippet, we import the `RouterModule` directly from `@angular/router`; as we can see, the router is externalized outside the framework's core. This module declares all the routing-specific directives, as well as all the routing-related providers, which means that, if we import it, we'll get access to all of them.

The `LocationStrategy` class is an abstract class that defines the common logic between `HashLocationStrategy` (used for hash-based routing) and `PathLocationStrategy` (used for HTML5-based routing by taking advantage of the history API).(that is, meaningful for the router).

 `HashLocationStrategy` does not support server-side rendering, because the hash of the page does not get sent to the server. Since the hash is our application's view identifier, the server will not be aware of the page that needs to be rendered. Fortunately, all modern browsers except IE9 support the HTML5 history API. You can find more about server-side rendering in the final chapter of this book.

Now, let's define a bootstrap component and configure the application's root module:

```
// ch6/ts/step-0/app.ts

@Component({
  selector: 'app',
  template: `...`,
  providers: [DeveloperCollection]
```

```
})
class App {}

const routeModule = RouterModule.forRoot([...]);

@NgModule({
  declarations: [App],
  bootstrap: [App],
  imports: [BrowserModule],
  providers: [{
    provide: LocationStrategy,
    useClass: HashLocationStrategy
  }]
})
class AppModule {}

platformBrowserDynamic().bootstrapModule(AppModule);
```

In the preceding snippet, we can notice a syntax we're already familiar with from Chapter 4, *Getting Started with Angular Components and Directives* and Chapter 5, *Dependency Injection in Angular*. We define a component with an app selector, template, which we will take a look at later, and sets of providers and directives.

The App component declares a single provider associated with the DeveloperCollection token. This is the class that contains all of the developers stored by the application. Later, we invoke the forRoot method of the RouterModule; this method allows us to configure the router by declaring some of the routes of the application.

Once we have imported the module, returned as a result of the invocation of forRoot, we already have access to a set of directives. These directives can help us link to the other routes defined as part of the router's configuration (the routerLink directive) and declare the place where the components associated with the different routes should be rendered (router-outlet). We'll explain how we can use them later in this section.

Now, let's take a look at the configuration of our AppModule:

```
@NgModule({
  declarations: [App],
  bootstrap: [App],
  imports: [BrowserModule, routeModule],
  providers: [{
    provide: LocationStrategy,
    useClass: HashLocationStrategy
  }]
})
class AppModule {}
```

We add a single declaration–the `App` component–that we use for bootstrapping the application. Note that, here, we import not only the `BrowserModule`, but also the result returned from the invocation of the `forRoot` method of the `RouterModule`. In the `providers` array, we configure the provider for the `LocationStrategy`. The default `LocationStrategy` implementation, which Angular uses, is `PathLocationStrategy` (that is, the HTML5-based one). However, in this case, we will use the hash-based one.

When we have to choose between the two location strategies, we should bear in mind that the default location strategy (`PathLocationStrategy`) is supported by the server-rendering module of Angular, and the application's URL looks more natural to the end user (there's no # used). On the other hand, if we use `PathLocationStrategy`, we may need to configure our application server in order to work with the HTML5 history API, which is not necessary for `HashLocationStrategy`.

Using PathLocationStrategy

The `PathLocationStrategy` uses `APP_BASE_HREF`, which by default has the string `"/"` as a value. This means that, in case the base pathname of our application is different, we must set it explicitly, in order to have a properly functioning location strategy. For instance, in our case, the configuration should look as follows:

```
import {APP_BASE_HREF} from '@angular/common';

//...
@NgModule({
  ...
  providers: [{
      provide: APP_BASE_HREF,
      useValue: '/dist/dev/ch6/ts/multi-page-template-driven/'
    },
    { provide: LocationStrategy, useClass: HashLocationStrategy }
  ]
})
class AppModule {}
```

`APP_BASE_HREF` represents the base path of the application. For instance, in our case, the "Coders repository" will be located under the `/dist/dev/ch6/ts/multi-page-template-driven/` directory (or, if we include the schema and the host, `http://localhost:5555/dist/dev/ch6/ts/multi-page-template-driven/`).

We will need to provide the value of APP_BASE_HREF in order to hint to Angular which part of the path is an application route (that is, meaningful for the router). For instance, for the URL

http://localhost:5555/dist/dev/ch6/ts/multi-page-template-driven/**home**, by having APP_BASE_HREF equal to /dist/dev/ch6/ts/multi-page-template-driven/, Angular will know that it needs to provide the component associated with the home path since the rest of the URL is not relevant to the declared routes within the application.

Configuring routes

As the next step, let's update the routes' declarations. Open ch6/ts/step-0/app.ts and update the invocation of the forRoot method of RouteModule:

```
// ch6/ts/step-1/app.ts

const routingModule = RouterModule.forRoot([
  {
    path: '',
    redirectTo: 'home',
    pathMatch: 'full'
  },
  {
    path: 'home',
    component: Home
  },
  {
    path: 'dev-add',
    component: AddDeveloper
  },
  {
    path: 'add-dev',
    redirectTo: 'dev-add'
  }
]);
```

As the preceding snippet shows, the method forRoot accepts an array of route declarations as an argument. We define two redirects and two routes with components associated with them.

Each non-lazy-loaded route must define the following properties:

- `component`: The component associated with the given route.
- `path`: The path to be used for the route — it will be visible in the browser's location bar.

On the other hand, the redirect's definition should contain:

- `path`: The path to be used for the redirection.
- `redirectTo`: The path the user will be redirected to.
- `pathMatch`: Defines the matching strategy.

In the previous example, we declare that when the user navigates to the path, we want `/add-dev` to be redirected to `/dev-add`. As we mentioned, `pathMatch` defines the path matching strategy. By default, it has the value `"prefix"`, which means that the router will try to match the beginning of the current route with the `path` property declared in the redirect. In contrast, when we set the `pathMatch` property to the value `"full"`, the router will redirect to the `redirectTo` path only when the entire path has been matched. It's important to explicitly set `pathMatch` to `"full"` in the first redirect, because otherwise every route will match the `""` path in case of a match by prefix.

Now, in order to make everything work, we will need to define the `AddDeveloper` and `Home` components, which are referenced in the router's configuration. First, we will provide a basic implementation that we'll incrementally extend over time, through the course of this chapter. In `ch6/ts/step-0`, create a file called `home.ts` and enter the following content:

```
import {Component} from '@angular/core';

@Component({
  selector: 'home',
  template: `Home`
})
export class Home {}
```

Now, open the file called `add_developer.ts`, and enter the following content in it:

```
import {Component} from '@angular/core';

@Component({
  selector: 'dev-add',
  template: `Add developer`
})
export class AddDeveloper {}
```

Do not forget to import the `Home` and `AddDeveloper` components in `app.ts`.

Using routerLink and router-outlet

We have the routes' declarations and all the components associated with them. The only thing left is to define the template of the root `App` component in order to link everything together.

Add the following content to the `template` property inside the `@Component` decorator in `ch6/ts/step-0/app.ts`:

```
@Component({
  //...
  template: `
    <nav class="navbar navbar-default">
      <ul class="nav navbar-nav">
        <li><a [routerLink]="['home']">Home</a></li>
        <li><a [routerLink]="['dev-add']">Add developer</a></li>
      </ul>
    </nav>
    <router-outlet></router-outlet>
  `,
  //...
})
```

In the template, there are two Angular-specific directives:

- `routerLink`: This allows us to add a link to a specific route.
- `router-outlet`: This defines the container where the components associated with the currently selected route should be rendered.

Let's take a look at the `routerLink` directive. As value, it accepts an array of route paths and parameters. In our case, we provide only a single route path. Note that the route name used by `routerLink` is declared by the `path` property of the route declaration inside `forRoot`. Later in this book, we'll see how we can link to nested routes and pass route parameters.

This directive allows us to declare links independently from the `LocationStrategy` that we configured. For instance, imagine we are using `HashLocationStrategy`; this means that we will need to prefix all the routes in our templates with `#`. In case we switch to

`PathLocationStrategy`, we'll need to remove all the hash prefixes. This is only a partial benefit of the neat abstraction that `routerLink` creates on top of path references.

The next directive that is new to us from the previous template is `router-outlet`. It has a similar responsibility to the `ng-view` directive in AngularJS. Basically, they both have the same role: to point out where the target component should be rendered. This means that, according to the definition, when the user navigates to /, the `Home` component will be rendered at the position pointed out by `router-outlet`, the same for the `AddDeveloper` component once the user navigates to `dev-add`.

Now, we have these two routes up and running! Open `http://localhost:5555/dist/dev/ch6/ts/step-0/`, and you should see a page which looks similar to the following screenshot:

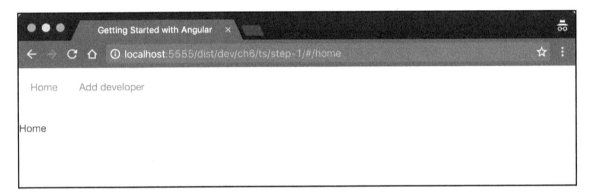

Figure 2

If you don't, just take a look at `ch6/ts/step-1` that contains the end result.

Lazy-loading with loadChildren

AngularJS modules allow us to group together logically related units in the application. However, by default, they need to be available during the initial application's bootstrap and do not allow deferred loading. This requires downloading the entire code base of the application during the initial page load that, in case of large single-page apps, can be an unacceptable performance hit.

In a perfect scenario, we would want to load only the code associated with the page the user is currently viewing or to prefetch bundled modules based on heuristics related to the user's behavior, which is out of the scope of this book. For instance, open the application from the first step of our example, `http://localhost:5555/dist/dev/ch6/ts/step-1/`. Once the user is at /, we only need the Home component to be available, and once they navigate to dev-add, we want to load the AddDeveloper component.

Let's inspect what is actually going on in Chrome DevTools:

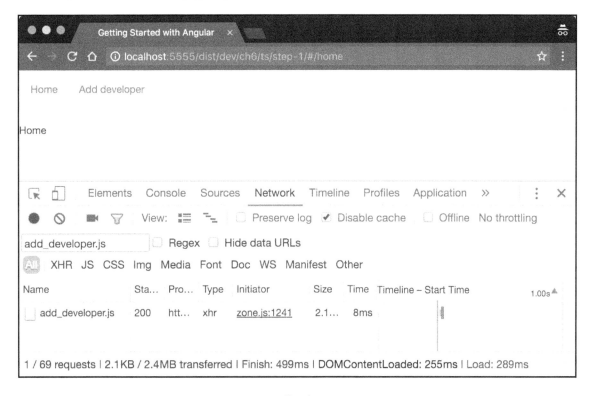

Figure 3

We can notice that during the initial page load, Angular downloads the components associated with all the routes, even AddDeveloper, which is not required. This happens because, in app.ts, we explicitly require both the Home and the AddDeveloper components and use them in the routes' declarations.

In this specific case, loading both components may not seem like a big problem because, at this step, they are pretty simple and do not have any dependencies. However, in real-life applications, they will have imports of other directives, components, pipes, services, or even third-party libraries. Once any of the components is required, its entire dependency graph will be downloaded, even if the component is not needed at that point.

The router of Angular comes with a solution to this problem:

```
// ch6/ts/step-1-async/app.ts

const routingModule = RouterModule.forRoot([
  {
    path: '',
    redirectTo: 'home',
    pathMatch: 'full'
  },
  {
    path: 'home',
    loadChildren: './home#HomeModule'
  },
  {
    path: 'dev-add',
    loadChildren: './add_developer#AddDeveloperModule'
  }
]);
```

The declaration of the lazy-loaded routes is an object with the following properties:

- `loadChildren`: A string that points to the path of the lazy-loaded module.
- `path`: The path of the route.

Once the user navigates to a route that matches any of the lazy-routes' definitions, a module loader (by default, SystemJS) will download the module from the location provided by `loadChildren`. When the promise returned by the loader is resolved with a value of the target module, the module will be cached and its bootstrap component will be rendered. The next time the user navigates to the same route, the cached module will be used, so the routing module won't download the same component twice.

Note the # symbol in the value of the `loadChildren` property. If we split the string by the # symbol, its first part will be the module's URL and its second part will be the name of the export that represents the Angular module the router will use for the route. If we don't provide a module name, Angular will use the default export.

The preceding example uses `loadChildren`, which by default loads modules with SystemJS. You can use a more advanced configuration and a custom module loader. For further information, take a look at the Angular documentation at http://angular.io.

Prefetching of lazy-loaded routes

As we have already mentioned, in the perfect scenario, we would want to download only the minimum set of resources that the user needs at a given time. For instance, if the user visits the home page, we'd want to download only the bundle that corresponds to the home module (i.e. `HomeModule`).

Later, when the user navigates to `dev-add`, the router will need to download the `AddDeveloperModule`. Although, this way, the user will consume network bandwidth only for the assets they use, the user experience will be far from perfect because of the slowdown that happens while navigating to as yet unvisited pages.

In order to handle this problem, we can add a route preloading strategy:

```
import {RouterModule, PreloadAllModules, ... } from '@angular/router';

...

export const appRoutes = RouterModule.forRoot(routes, {
  preloadingStrategy: PreloadAllModules
});
```

In the preceding snippet, we declare that we want to use the default `preloadingStrategy` that Angular provides. As a result, when the user opens `home` and the `HomeModule` is successfully downloaded, the router will automatically start prefetching all the other routes. So, next time, when the user navigates to a different page, it will most likely be already available in-memory. This will introduce a neat improvement to the user experience at almost no cost.

By providing a custom implementation of the abstract class `PreloadingStrategy` (located in the `@angular/router` package), we can introduce a custom mechanism for the prefetching of lazy-loaded modules.

RouterModule.forRoot versus RouterModule.forChild

There are two methods we can invoke using the `RouterModule` in order to register routes.

In case we declare the top-level routes of our application, we need to use `RouterModule.forRoot`. This method will register the top-level routes and return the routing module that should be imported by the application's root module.

If we want to define routes in a lazy-loaded module and import the module returned by the invocation of the `forRoot` method, we'll get a runtime error. This is because the `forRoot` method will return a module with providers, which should be imported only once, by the top-level module. In order to register nested routes in a lazy-loaded module, we will need to use the `forChild` method.

We'll take a further look at how we can define nested routes in Chapter 7, *Explaining Pipes and Communicating with RESTful Services*.

 As a rule of thumb, we can remember that `RouterModule.forRoot` is meant for the registration of top-level routes, and `RouterModule.forChild` should be used only for the registration of nested routes in a lazy-loaded module.

Using Angular's forms module

Now, let's continue with the implementation of the application. For the next step, we'll work on the `AddDeveloper` and `Home` components. You can continue your implementation by extending what you currently have in `ch6/ts/step-0`, or if you haven't reached step 1 yet, you can keep working on the files in `ch6/ts/step-1`.

Angular offers two ways of developing forms with validation:

- **A template-driven approach**: This provides a declarative API where we declare the validations into the template of the component.
- **A model-driven approach (also known as reactive forms)**: This provides an imperative, reactive API.

Let's start with the template-driven approach for now and explore the model-driven approach in the next chapter.

Developing template-driven forms

Forms are essential for each **CRUD (Create Retrieve Update and Delete)** application. In our case, we want to build a form for entering the details of the developers we want to store.

By the end of this section, we'll have a form that allows us to enter the real name of a given developer, to add their preferred technology, enter their e-mail, and declare whether they are popular in the community or not yet. The end result will look as follows:

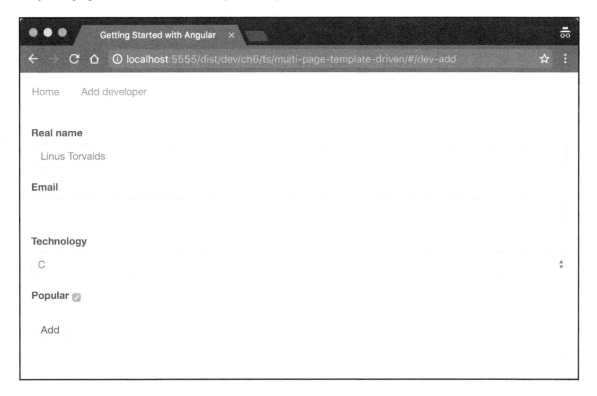

Figure 4

Add the following import to `app.ts`:

```
import {FormsModule} from '@angular/forms';
```

The next thing we need to do is import `FormsModule` in our `AppModule`. The `FormsModule` contains a set of predefined directives for managing Angular forms, such as the `form` and `ngModel` directives. The `FormsModule` also declares an array with a predefined set of form-related providers that we can use in our application.

After the import of the `FormsModule`, our `app.ts` will look like:

```
// ch6/ts/step-2/add_developer.ts

@NgModule({
  imports: [BrowserModule, FormsModule, routingModule],
```

```
    declarations: [App, Home, AddDeveloper, ControlErrors],
    providers: [{
      provide: LocationStrategy,
      useClass: HashLocationStrategy
    }],
    bootstrap: [App]
})
class AppModule {}
```

Now, update the `AddDeveloper` implementation to the following:

```
// ch6/ts/step-2/add_developer.ts

@Component({
  selector: 'dev-add',
  templateUrl: './add_developer.html',
  styles: [...]
})
export class AddDeveloper {
  developer = new Developer();
  errorMessage: string;
  successMessage: string;
  submitted = false;
  // ...
  constructor(private developers: DeveloperCollection) {}
  addDeveloper() {}
}
```

The `developer` property contains the information associated with the current developer that we're adding with the form. The last two properties, `errorMessage` and `successMessage`, will be used respectively to display the current form's error or success messages once the developer has been successfully added to the developers collection, or when an error has occurred.

Digging into the template-driven form's markup

As the next step, let's create the template for the `AddDeveloper` component (`step-1/add_developer.html`). Add the following content to the file:

```
<span *ngIf="errorMessage"
      class="alert alert-danger">{{errorMessage}}</span>
<span *ngIf="successMessage"
      class="alert alert-success">{{successMessage}}</span>
```

These two elements are intended to display the error and success messages when you add a new developer. They will be visible when `errorMessage` or `successMessage` have non-falsy values (that is, something different from the empty string, `false`, `undefined`, `0`, `NaN`, or `null`).

Now, let's develop the actual form:

```
<form #f="ngForm" class="form col-md-4" [hidden]="submitted"
   (ngSubmit)="addDeveloper()">
  <div class="form-group">
    <label class="control-label" for="realNameInput">Real name</label>
    <div>
      <input id="realNameInput" class="form-control"
          type="text" name="realName"
          [(ngModel)]="developer.realName" required>
    </div>
  </div>
  <!-- MORE CODE TO BE ADDED -->
  <button class="btn btn-default" type="submit">Add</button>
</form>
```

We declare a new form using the HTML `form` tag. Once Angular finds such tags in a template with an included form directive in the parent component, it will automatically enhance its functionality in order to be used as an Angular form. Once the form is processed by Angular, we can apply form validation and data bindings. After this, using `#f="ngForm"`, we define a local variable in template, which allows us to reference to the form using the identifier `f`. The last thing left from the form element is the submit event handler. We use a syntax that we're already familiar with, `(ngSubmit)="expr"`; in this case, the value of the expression is the call of the `addDeveloper` method defined in the component's controller.

Now, let's take a look at the `div` element with the class name `control-group`.

> Note that this is not an Angular-specific class; it is a CSS class defined by Bootstrap that we use in order to provide a better look and feel to the form.

Inside the `div` element, we can find a `label` element that doesn't have any Angular-specific markup and an input element that allows us to set the real name of the current developer. We set the control to be of a type text and declare its identifier and name equal to `realNameInput`. The `required` attribute is defined by the HTML5 specification and is used for validation. By using it on the element, we declare that this element is required to have a value. Although the `required` attribute is not Angular-specific, Angular will extend its semantics by including an Angular-specific validation behavior. This behavior includes setting specific CSS classes on the control when its status changes and managing its state which the framework keeps internally.

The behavior of the form controls will be enhanced by running validation over them when their values change, and applying specific classes during the controls' life cycles. You may be familiar with this from AngularJS, where the form controls are decorated with the `ng-pristine`, `ng-invalid`, and `ng-valid` classes, and so on.

The following table summarizes the CSS classes that the framework adds to the form controls during their life cycle:

Classes	Description
`ng-untouched`	The control hasn't been visited
`ng-touched`	The control has been visited
`ng-pristine`	The control's value hasn't been changed
`ng-dirty`	The control's value has been changed
`ng-valid`	All the validators attached to the control have returned `true`
`ng-invalid`	Any of the validators attached to the control has a `false` value

According to this table, we can define that we want all the input controls with an invalid value to have a red border in the following way:

```
input.ng-dirty.ng-invalid {
  border: 1px solid red;
}
```

The exact semantics behind the preceding CSS in the context of Angular is that we use a red border for all the input elements whose values were changed and are invalid according to the validators attached to them.

Now, let's explore how we can attach validation behavior to our controls.

Using the built-in validators

We have already seen that we can alter validation behavior to any control using the `required` attribute. Angular provides two more built-in validators, as follows:

- `minlength`: This allows us to specify the minimum length of value that a given control should have.
- `maxlength`: This allows us to specify the maximum length of value that a given control should have.

These validators are defined with Angular directives and can be used in the following way:

```
<input id="realNameInput" class="form-control"
       type="text" minlength="2" maxlength="30">
```

This way, we specify that we want the value of the input to be between 2 and 30 characters.

Defining custom validators

Another data property defined in the `Developer` class is `email`. Let's add an input field for it. Above the **Add** button in the preceding form, add the following markup:

```
<div class="form-group">
  <label class="control-label" for="emailInput">Email</label>
  <div>
    <input type="text" id="emailInput" class="form-control"
name="emailInput"
           [(ngModel)]="developer.email">
  </div>
</div>
```

We can think of the `[(ngModel)]` as an alternative to the `ng-model` directive from AngularJS. We will explain it in detail in the *Two-way data binding with Angular* section.

Although Angular provides a set of predefined validators, they are not enough for all the various formats our data can live in. Sometimes, we'll need custom validation logic for our application-specific data. For instance, in this case, we want to define an e-mail validator. A typical regular expression, which works in general cases (but does not cover the entire specification that defines the format of the e-mail addresses), looks as follows: `/^[a-zA-Z0-9_.+-]+@[a-zA-Z0-9-]+\.[a-zA-Z0-9-.]+$/`.

In `ch6/ts/step-1/email_validator.ts`, define a function that accepts an instance of Angular control as an argument and returns `null` if the control's value is empty or matches the regular expression mentioned earlier, and `{ 'invalidEmail': true }` otherwise:

```
function validateEmail(emailControl) {
  if (!emailControl.value ||
    /^[a-zA-Z0-9_.+-]+@[a-zA-Z0-9-]+\.[a-zA-Z0-9-
.]+$/.test(emailControl.value)) {
    return null;
  } else {
    return { 'invalidEmail': true };
  }
}
```

Now, from the `@angular/common` and `@angular/core` modules, import `NG_VALIDATORS` and `Directive`, and wrap this validation function within the following directive:

```
@Directive({
  selector: '[email-input]',
  providers: [{
    provide: NG_VALIDATORS,
    multi: true,
    useValue: validateEmail
  }]
})
class EmailValidator {}
```

In the preceding code, we defined a multiprovider for the token `NG_VALIDATORS`. Once we inject the value associated with this token, we'll get an array with all the validators attached to the given control (for reference, take a look at the section for multiproviders in Chapter 5, *Dependency Injection in Angular*).

There are only two steps left in order to make our custom validation work. First, add the `email-input` attribute to the e-mail control:

```
<input type="text" id="emailInput" class="form-control" email-input
       [(ngModel)]="developer.email">
```

Next, add the directive to the declarations in the `AppModule`:

```
// ...
import {EmailValidator} from './email_validator';
// ...

@NgModule({
  // ...
  declarations: [..., EmailValidator],
```

```
  // ...
})
class AppModule {}
```

We're using an external template for the `AddDeveloper` control. There's no ultimate answer to whether a given template should be externalized or inlined. Best practice states that we should inline the short templates and externalize the longer ones. However, there's no specific definition as to which templates are considered short and which are considered long. The decision of whether the template should be used inline or put into an external file depends on the developer's personal preferences or common conventions within the organization.

Using select inputs with Angular

As the next step, we should allow the user of the application to enter the technology into which the input developer has the most proficiency. We can define a list of technologies and show them in the form as a select input.

In the `AddDeveloper` class, add the `technologies` property:

```
class AddDeveloper {
  ...
  technologies: string[] = [
    'JavaScript',
    'C',
    'C#',
    'Clojure'
  ];
  ...
}
```

Now, in the template, just above the **Add** button, add the following markup:

```
<div class="form-group">
  <label class="control-label"
        for="technologyInput">Technology</label>
  <div>
    <select class="form-control" name="technology" required
            [(ngModel)]="developer.technology">
      <option *ngFor="let technology of technologies"
[value]="technology">
        {{technology}}
      </option>
    </select>
```

```
    </div>
  </div>
```

Just like for the input elements we declared earlier, Angular will add the same classes depending on the state of the select input. In order to show a red border around the select element when its value is invalid, we will need to alter the CSS rules:

```
@Component({
  ...
  styles: [
    `input.ng-touched.ng-invalid,
     select.ng-touched.ng-invalid {
      border: 1px solid red;
    }`
  ],
  ...
})
class AddDeveloper {...}
```

 Note that inlining all the styles in our components' declaration could be a bad practice because, this way, they won't be reusable. What we can do is extract all the common styles across our components into separate files. The @Component decorator has a property called styleUrls of type string[] where we can add a reference to the extracted styles used by the given component. This way, we can inline only the component-specific styles, if required.

Right after this, we declare the name of the control to be equal to "technology" using name="technology". Using the required attribute, we declare that the user of the application must specify the technology in which the current developer is proficient. Let's skip the [(ngModel)] attribute for now and see how we can define the options of the select element.

Inside the select element, we define the different options using:

```
<option *ngFor="let technology of technologies" [value]="technology">
  {{technology}}
</option>
```

This is a syntax we're already familiar with. We simply iterate over all the technologies defined within the AddDeveloper class, and for each technology we show an option element with a value for the technology name.

Using the NgForm directive

We have already mentioned that the form directive enhances the HTML5 form's behavior by adding some additional Angular-specific logic. Now, let's take a step back and take a look at the form that surrounds the input elements:

```
<form #f="ngForm" (ngSubmit)="addDeveloper()"
      class="form col-md-4" [hidden]="submitted">
  ...
</form>
```

In the preceding snippet, we define a new identifier called `f`, which references to the form. We can think of the form as a composition of controls; we can access the individual controls through the form's `controls` property. On top of this, the form has the **touched**, **untouched**, **pristine**, **dirty**, **invalid**, and **valid** properties, which depend on the individual controls defined within the form. For example, if none of the controls within the form have been touched, then the form itself will show untouched as its status. However, if any of the controls in the form have been touched at least once, the form will show as touched. Similarly, the form will be valid only if all its controls are valid.

In order to illustrate the usage of the `form` element, let's define a component with the `control-errors` selector, which shows the current errors for a given control. We can use it in the following way:

```
<label class="control-label" for="realNameInput">Real name</label>
<div>
  <input id="realNameInput" class="form-control" type="text"
         [(ngModel)]="developer.realName"
         required maxlength="50">
  <control-errors control="realName"
    [errors]="{
      'required': 'Real name is required',
      'maxlength': 'The maximum length of the real name is 50 characters'
    }"
  />
</div>
```

Note that we've also added the `maxlength` validator to the `realName` control.

The `control-errors` element has the following attributes:

- `control`: This declares the name of the control we want to show errors for.
- `errors`: This creates a mapping between control error and an error message.

Now, create a new file called `control_errors.ts` and add the following imports in it:

```
import {Component, Host, Input} from '@angular/core';
import {NgForm} from '@angular/forms';
```

In these imports, `NgForm` represents the Angular forms, and `Host` is a parameter decorator related to the DI mechanism, which we have already covered in `Chapter 5`, *Dependency Injection in Angular*.

Here is a part of the component's definition:

```
@Component({
  template: '<div>{{currentError}}</div>',
  selector: 'control-errors',
})
class ControlErrors {
  @Input() errors: Object;
  @Input() control: string;
  constructor(@Host() private formDir: NgForm) {}
  get currentError() {...}
}
```

The `ControlErrors` component defines two inputs: `control`, the name of the control (the value of the `name` attribute) and `errors`, the mapping between an error identifier and an error message. They can be specified, respectively, by the `control` and the `errors` attributes of the `control-errors` element.

For instance, lets suppose we have the following input:

```
<input type="text" name="foobar" required>
```

We can declare its associated `control-errors` component using the following markup:

```
<control-errors control="foobar"
      [errors]="{
       'required': 'The value of foobar is required'
      }"></control-errors>
```

Inside the `currentError` getter, in the declaration of the `ControlErrors` class above, we need to do the following two things:

- Find a reference to the component declared with the `control` attribute.
- Return the error message associated with any of the errors that make the current control invalid.

Here is a snippet that implements this behavior:

```
@Component(...)
class ControlErrors {
  ...
  get currentError() {
    let control = this.formDir.controls[this.control];
    let errorMessages = [];
    if (control && control.touched) {
      errorMessages = Object.keys(this.errors)
        .map(k => control.hasError(k) ? this.errors[k] : null)
        .filter(error => !!error);
    }
    return errorMessages.pop();
  }
}
```

In the first line of the implementation of `currentError`, we get the target control using the `controls` property of the injected form. The `controls` property is of the type `{[key: string]: AbstractControl}`, where the `key` is the name of the control we've declared with the `name` attribute. Once we have a reference to the instance of the target control, we can check whether its status is touched (that is, whether it has been focused), and if it is, we can loop over all the errors within the `errors` property of the instance of `ControlErrors`. The `map` function will return an array with either an error message or a `null` value. The only thing left to do is to filter all the `null` values and get only the error messages. Once we get the error messages for each error, we will return the last one by popping it from the `errorMessages` array.

The end result should look as follows:

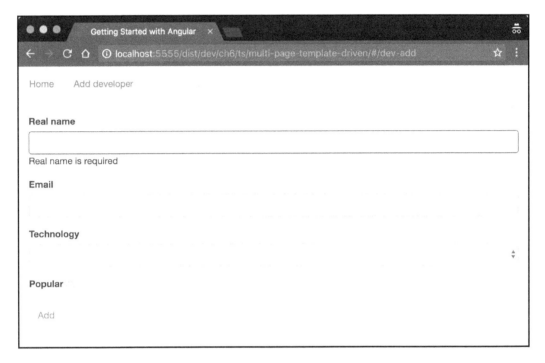

Figure 5

If you experience any problems during the implementation of the
`ControlErrors` component, you can take a look at its implementation at
`ch6/ts/step-2/control_errors.ts`.

The `hasError` method of every control accepts as an argument an error message identifier,
which is defined by the corresponding validator. For instance, in the preceding example,
where we defined the custom e-mail validator, we return the `{ 'invalidEmail': true
}` object literal when the input control has an invalid value. If we apply the `ControlErrors`
component to the e-mail control, its declaration should look as follows:

```
<control-errors control="email"
  [errors]="{
    'invalidEmail': 'Invalid email address'
  }"></control-errors>
```

Two-way data binding with Angular

One of the most famous rumors about Angular 2 was that the two-way data binding functionality was removed because of the enforced unidirectional data flow. This is not exactly true; the Angular's form module implements a directive with the selector `[(ngModel)]` (we'll also refer to this directive as `NgModel`, because of the name of its controller), which allows us to easily achieve data binding in two directions: from the view to the model and from the model to the view.

Let's take a look at the following simple component:

```
// ch6/ts/simple-two-way-data-binding/app.ts

import {Component, NgModule} from '@angular/core';
import {BrowserModule} from '@angular/platform-browser';
import {FormsModule} from '@angular/forms';
import {platformBrowserDynamic} from '@angular/platform-browser-dynamic';

@Component({
  selector: 'app',
  template: `
   <input type="text" [(ngModel)]="name">
   <div>{{name}}</div>
  `
})
class App {
  name: string;
}

@NgModule({
  imports: [BrowserModule, FormsModule],
  declarations: [App],
  bootstrap: [App]
})
class AppModule {}

platformBrowserDynamic().bootstrapModule(AppModule);
```

In the preceding example, we import the `FormsModule` from the `@angular/common` package. Later, in the template, we set the attribute `[(ngModel)]` to `name`.

At first, the `[(ngModel)]` syntax might seem a little bit unusual. From Chapter 4, *Getting Started with Angular Components and Directives*, we know that the `(eventName)` syntax is used for binding to events (or outputs) triggered by a given component. On the other hand, we use the `[propertyName]="foobar"` syntax to achieve one-way data binding by setting the value of the property (or, in the terminology of the Angular components, the input) with the name `propertyName` to the result of the evaluation of the expression `foobar`. The `[(ngModel)]` syntax combines both in order to achieve data binding in two directions. That's why we can think of it more like a syntax sugar, rather than a new concept. One of the main advantages of this syntax compared to AngularJS is that we can tell which bindings are one-way and which are two-way by just looking at the template.

 Another name of the `[(foo)]` syntax is "banana in a box" or "banana brackets" syntax. The source of this term is the paper *Functional Programming with Bananas, Lenses, Envelopes and Barbed Wire* by *Erik Meijer, Maarten Fokkinga*, and *Ross Paterson* (`http://eprints.eemcs.utwente.nl /7281/01/db-utwente-40501F46.pdf`).

Just like `(click)` has its canonical syntax `on-click`, and `[propertyName]` has its own `bind-propertyName`, the alternative syntax of `[(ngModel)]` is `bindon-ngModel`.

If you open `http://localhost:5555/dist/dev/ch6/ts/simple-two-way-data-binding/`, you will see the following result:

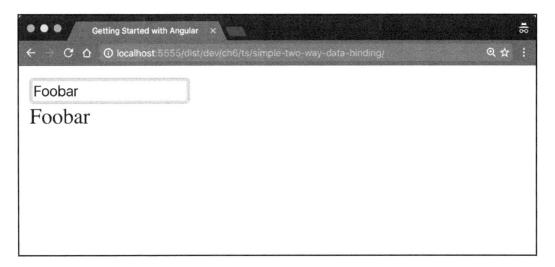

Figure 6

Once the value of the input box is changed, the label below it will update automatically.

We have already used the `[(ngModel)]` directive in the previous snippets. For example, we bound to the developer's e-mail using:

```
<input id="emailInput" class="form-control" type="text"
       [(ngModel)]="developer.email" email-input>
```

This way, the value of the e-mail property of the developer object defined in the `AddDeveloper` component's instance will be updated once we change the value of the text input.

Storing the form data

Let's peek at the interface of the `AddDeveloper` component's controller again:

```
export class AddDeveloper {
  submitted: false;
  successMessage: string;
  developer = new Developer();
  //...
  constructor(private developers: DeveloperCollection) {}
  addDeveloper(form) {...}
}
```

It has a field of the `Developer` type, and we bind the form controls to its properties using the `NgModel` directive. The class also has a method called `addDeveloper`, which is being invoked on the submission of the form. We declare this by binding to the `ngSubmit` event using:

```
<!-- ch6/ts/multi-page-template-driven/add_developer.html -->
<form #f="form" (ngSubmit)="addDeveloper()"
      class="form col-md-4" [hidden]="submitted">

  ...
  <button class="btn btn-default"
      type="submit" [disabled]="!f.form.valid">Add</button>
</form>
```

In the preceding snippet, we can note two more things. We got a reference to the form using `#f="ngForm"` and bound the disabled property of the button to the `!f.form.valid` expression. We have already described the `NgForm` control in the previous section; its `valid` property will have a value `true` once all the controls within the form have valid values.

Now, let's suppose we've entered valid values for all the input controls in the form. This means that its submit button will be enabled. Once we press *Enter* or click on the submit button, the `addDeveloper` method will be invoked. The following is a sample implementation of this method:

```
class AddDeveloper {
  //...
  addDeveloper() {
    // We can't remove developers so setting the id this way is safe
    this.developer.id = this.developers.getAll().length + 1;
    this.developers.addDeveloper(this.developer);
    this.successMessage = `Developer ${this.developer.realName} was
successfully added`;
    this.submitted = true;
  }
}
```

Initially, we set the `id` property of the current developer equal to the total number of developers in `DeveloperCollection`, plus one. Later, we add the developer to the collection and set the value of the `successMessage` property. Right after this, we set the property submitted equal to `true`, which will result in hiding the form.

Listing all the stored data

Now that we can add a new entry to the developers' collection, let's show a list of all the developers on the front page of the "Coders repository".

Open the file `ch6/ts/step-1/home.ts` (or step-2, depending on your progress during the past section), and enter the following content:

```
import {Component} from '@angular/core';
import {DeveloperCollection} from './developer_collection';

@Component({
  selector: 'home',
  templateUrl: './home.html'
})
export class Home {
  constructor(private developers: DeveloperCollection) {}

  getDevelopers() {
    return this.developers.getAll();
  }
}
```

There is nothing new to us here. We extend the functionality of the `Home` component by providing an external template and implementing the `getDevelopers` method, which delegates its call to the instance of `DeveloperCollection` that is injected in the constructor.

The template itself is something that we're already familiar with:

```
<table class="table" *ngIf="getDevelopers().length > 0">
  <thead>
    <th>Email</th>
    <th>Real name</th>
    <th>Technology</th>
    <th>Popular</th>
  </thead>
  <tr *ngFor="let dev of getDevelopers()">
    <td>{{dev.email}}</td>
    <td>{{dev.realName}}</td>
    <td>{{dev.technology}}</td>
    <td [ngSwitch]="dev.popular">
      <span *ngSwitchCase="true">Yes</span>
      <span *ngSwitchCase="false">Not yet</span>
    </td>
  </tr>
</table>
<div *ngIf="getDevelopers().length == 0">
  There are no any developers yet
</div>
```

We list all the developers as rows within an HTML table. For each developer, we check the status of its `popular` flag. If its value is `true`, then for the **Popular** column, we show a span with the text `Yes`, otherwise we set the text to `No`.

When you enter a few developers in the **Add developer** page and then navigate to the home page, you should see a result similar to the following screenshot:

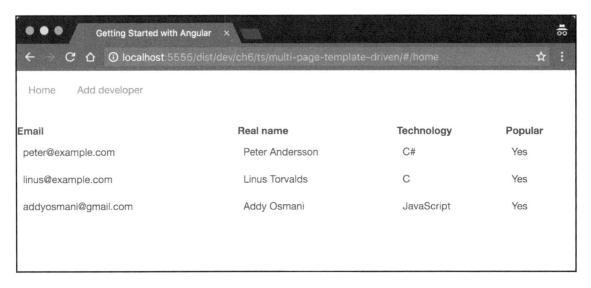

Figure 7

You can find the complete functionalities of the application at
`ch6/ts/multi-page-template-driven`.

Summary

So far, we have explained the basics of routing in Angular. We took a look at how we can define different routes and implement the components associated with them that are displayed on route change. In order to link to the different routes, we introduced `routerLink`, and we also used the `router-outlet` directives for pointing out where the components associated with the individual routes should be rendered.

Another thing we took a look at was the Angular forms functionality with built-in and custom validation. After this, we explained the `NgModel` directive, which provides us with two-way data binding.

In the next chapter, we will cover how we can develop model-driven forms, child and parameterized routes, use the `Http` module for making RESTful calls, and transform data with custom pipes.

7
Explaining Pipes and Communicating with RESTful Services

In the last chapter, we covered some very powerful features of the framework. However, we can go even deeper into the functionality of Angular's forms module and router. In the next sections, we'll explain how we can:

- Develop model-driven forms.
- Define parameterized routes.
- Define child routes.
- Use the HTTP module for communication with RESTful APIs.
- Transform data with custom pipes.

We will explore all these concepts in the process of extending the functionality of the "Coders repository" application. At the beginning of the preceding chapter, we mentioned that we will allow the import of developers from GitHub. However, before we implement this feature, let's extend the functionality of the form.

Developing model-driven forms in Angular

These will be the last steps for finishing the "Coders repository". You can build on top of the code available at `ch6/ts/step-1/` (or `ch6/ts/step-2`, depending on your previous work), in order to extend the application's functionality with the new concepts we will cover. The complete example is located at `ch7/ts/multi-page-model-driven`.

This is the result that we will achieve by the end of this section:

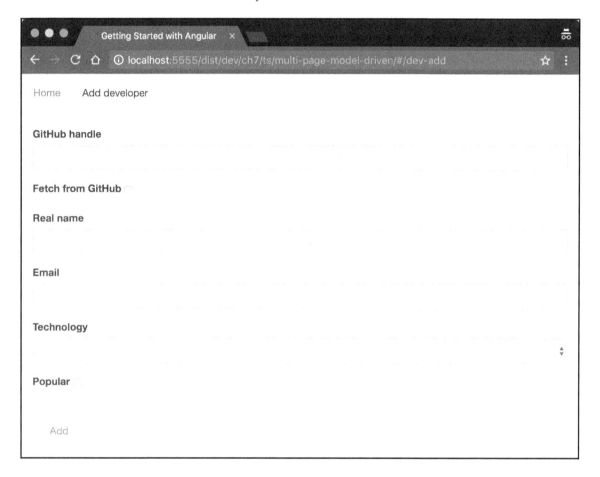

Figure 1

In the preceding screenshot, there are two forms:

- A form that contains the following controls for importing existing users from GitHub:
    - The input for the GitHub handle.
    - A checkbox that points out whether we want to import the developer from GitHub or enter it manually.
- A form for entering new users manually.

The second form looks exactly the way we left it in the last chapter. However, this time, its definition looks a little bit different:

```
<form class="form col-md-4" [formGroup]="addDevForm" [hidden]="submitted">
  <!-- TODO -->
</form>
```

Note that, this time, we don't have the `submit` handler or the `#f="ngForm"` attribute. Instead, we bind the `[formGroup]` property to `addDevForm` defined inside the component's controller. Using this attribute, we can bind to something called `FormGroup`. As its name states, the `FormGroup` class consists of a list of controls grouped together with the sets of validation rules associated with them.

We need to use a similar declaration in the form used for importing a developer. However, this time, we will provide a different value of the `[formGroup]` property, as we will define a different form group in the component's controller. Place the following snippet above the form we introduced earlier:

```
<form class="form col-md-4" [formGroup]="importDevForm"
[hidden]="submitted">
<!-- TODO -->
</form>
```

Now, let's declare the `importDevForm` and `addDevForm` properties in the component's controller:

```
import {FormGroup} from '@angular/forms';

@Component(...)
export class AddDeveloper {
  importDevForm: FormGroup;
  addDevForm: FormGroup;
  ...
  constructor(private developers: DeveloperCollection,
    fb: FormBuilder) {...}
  addDeveloper() {...}
}
```

Initially, we import the `FormGroup` class from the `@angular/forms` module and, later, declare the required properties in the controller. Note that we have one additional parameter of the constructor of `AddDeveloper` called `fb` of the `FormBuilder` type.

`FormBuilder` provides a programmable API for the definition of `FormGroup` where we can attach validation behavior to each control in the group. Let's use the `FormBuilder` instance for the initialization of the `importDevForm` and `addDevForm` properties:

```
. . .
constructor(private developers: DeveloperCollection,
  fb: FormBuilder) {
  this.importDevForm = fb.group({
    githubHandle: ['', Validators.required],
    fetchFromGitHub: [false]
  });
  this.addDevForm = fb.group({
    realName: ['', Validators.required],
    email: ['', validateEmail],
    technology: ['', Validators.required],
    popular: [false]
  });
}
. . .
```

The `FormBuilder` instance has a method called `group` that allows us to define properties, such as the default values and the validators for the individual controls in a given form.

According to the previous snippet, `importDevForm` has two fields: `githubHandle` and `fetchFromGitHub`. We declare that the value of the `githubHandle` control is required, and set the default value of the control `fetchFromGitHub` to `false`.

In the second form, `addDevForm`, we declare four controls. For the `realName` control as the default value, we set the empty string and use `Validators.requred` in order to introduce validation behavior (which is exactly what we did for the `githubHandle` control). As a validator for the e-mail input, we will use the `validateEmail` function and set the control's initial value to an empty string. The `validateEmail` function used for validation is the one we defined in the last chapter:

```
function validateEmail(emailControl) {
  if (!emailControl.value ||
      /^[a-zA-Z0-9_.+-]+@[a-zA-Z0-9-]+\.[a-zA-Z0-9-
.]+$/.test(emailControl.value)) {
    return null;
  } else {
    return { 'invalidEmail': true };
  }
}
```

The last two controls we define here are the `technology` control, for which a value is required and has an empty string as its initial value, and the `popular` control, with its initial value set to `false`.

Using composition of control validators

We took a look at how we can apply a single validator to form controls. Using model-driven approach, we applied the `Validators.required` validator in a way equivalent to what we did in the preceding chapter, where we used template-driven forms and added the `required` attribute. However, in some applications, the domain may require a more complex validation logic. For example, if we want to apply both the required and the `validateEmail` validators to the e-mail control, we should do the following:

```
this.addDevForm = fb.group({
  ...
  email: ['', Validators.compose([
    Validators.required,
    validateEmail]
  )],
  ...
});
```

The `compose` method of the `Validators` object accepts an array of validators as an argument and returns a new validator. The new validator's behavior will be a composition of the logic defined in the individual validators passed as an argument, and they will be applied in the same order as they were introduced in the array.

The property names in the object literal passed to the `group` method, of the `FormBuilder`, should match with the values that we set to the `formControlName` attributes of the inputs in the template. This is the complete template of `importDevForm`:

```
<form class="form col-md-4" [formGroup]="importDevForm"
[hidden]="submitted">
  <div class="form-group">
  <label class="control-label" for="githubHandleInput">GitHub
handle</label>
  <div>
    <input id="githubHandleInput" class="form-control"
          type="text" formControlName="githubHandle">
    <control-errors control="githubHandle"
      [errors]="{
        'required': 'The GitHub handle is required'
      }"></control-errors>
```

```
    </div>
    </div>
    <div class="form-group">
      <label class="control-label" for="fetchFromGitHubCheckbox">
        Fetch from GitHub
      </label>
      <input class="checkbox-inline" id="fetchFromGitHubCheckbox"
        type="checkbox" formControlName="fetchFromGitHub">
    </div>
  </form>
```

In the preceding template, we can note that, once the `submitted` flag has the value `true`, the form will be hidden from the user. Next to the first input element, we will set the value of the `formControlName` attribute to `githubHandle`. The `formControlName` attribute associates an existing form input in the template with one declared in the `FormGroup`, corresponding to the form element where HTML input resides. This means that the key associated with the controls' definition inside the object literal, which we pass to the `group` method of the `FormBuilder`, must match with the name of the corresponding control in the template, set with `formControlName`.

Now we want to implement the following behavior:

- When the **Fetch from GitHub** checkbox is checked, disable the form for entering a new developer and enable the form for importing a developer from GitHub.
- When the current active (or enabled) form is invalid, disable the submit button.

We'll explore how we can achieve this functionality using Angular's reactive forms (also known as model-driven forms) API.

Inside the `AddDeveloper` class, add the following methods definitions:

```
...
export class AddDeveloper {
  //...
  ngOnInit() {

  this.toggleControls(this.importDevForm.controls['fetchFromGitHub'].value);
    this.subscription = this.importDevForm.controls['fetchFromGitHub']
      .valueChanges.subscribe(this.toggleControls.bind(this));
  }

  ngOnDestroy() {
    this.subscription.unsubscribe();
  }

  private toggleControls(importEnabled: boolean) {
```

```
      const addDevControls = this.addDevForm.controls;
      if (importEnabled) {
        this.importDevForm.controls['githubHandle'].enable();
        Object.keys(addDevControls).forEach((c: string) =>
          addDevControls[c].disable());
      } else {
        this.importDevForm.controls['githubHandle'].disable();
        Object.keys(addDevControls).forEach((c: string) =>
          addDevControls[c].enable());
      }
    }
  }
  ...
```

Note that in `ngOnInit`, we invoke the `toggleControls` method with the current value of the `fetchFromGitHub` checkbox. We can get reference to the `AbstractControl`, which represents the checkbox, by getting the `fetchFromGitHub` property of the `controls` within the `importDevForm`.

After that, we subscribe to the `valueChange` event of the checkbox by passing a callback to its `subscribe` method. Each time the value of the checkbox is changed, the callback we've passed to `subscribe` will be invoked.

Later, in `ngOnDestroy`, we unsubscribe from the `valueChange` subscription in order to prevent our code from memory leaks.

Finally, the most interesting thing happens in `toggleControls`. To this method, we pass a flag that indicates whether we want the `importDevForm` to be enabled or not. If we want the form to be enabled, all we need to do is to invoke the `enable` method of the `githubHandle` control and disable all the controls in the `addDevForm`. We can disable all the controls in `addDevForm` by iterating over the control names (that is, the keys of the `controls` property of the `addDevForm`), getting the corresponding control instance for each individual name, and invoking its disable method. In case the `importEnabled` flag has value `false`, we do the exact opposite, by invoking the `enable` method of the controls from the `addDevForm` and the `disable` method of the control from `importDevForm`.

Exploring the HTTP module of Angular

Now, after we have developed both forms — for importing existing and adding new developers, it is time to implement the logic behind them in the controller of the component.

For this purpose, we will need to communicate with the GitHub API. Although we can do this directly from the component's controller, by approaching the problem this way, we would couple the component with the RESTful API of GitHub. In order to enforce better separation of concerns, we can extract the logic for communication with GitHub into a separate service called GitHubGateway. Open the file called github_gateway.ts, and enter the following content:

```
import {Injectable} from '@angular/core';
import {Http} from '@angular/http';

@Injectable()
export class GitHubGateway {
  constructor(private http: Http) {}

  getUser(username: string) {
    return this.http
      .get(`https://api.github.com/users/${username}`);
  }
}
```

Initially, we import the Http class from the @angular/http module. All the HTTP-related functionalities are externalized and are outside the Angular's core. Since GitHubGateway accepts a dependency, which needs to be injected through the DI mechanism of the framework, we will decorate it with the @Injectable decorator.

The only functionality from the GitHub's API we use is the one for fetching users, so we define a single method called getUser. As an argument, it accepts the GitHub handle of the developer.

 Note that, if you make more than 60 requests per day to the GitHub's API, you might get the error **GitHub API Rate limit exceeded**. This is due to the rate limits for requests without a GitHub API token. For further information, visit https://github.com/blog/1509-personal-api-tokens.

Inside the getUser method, we use the instance of the Http service that we received in the constructor. The Http service's API stays as close to the HTML5 fetch API as possible. However, there are a couple of differences. The most significant one of them is that, at the moment of writing this content, all the methods of the Http instances return Observables instead of Promises.

The `Http` service instances have the following API:

- `request(url: string | Request, options: RequestOptionsArgs)`: This makes a request to the specified URL. The request can be configured using `RequestOptionsArgs`, as follows:

```
http.request('http://example.com/', {
  method: 'get',
  search: 'foo=bar',
  headers: new Headers({
    'X-Custom-Header': 'Hello'
  })
});
```

- `get(url: string, options?: RequestOptionsArgs)`: This makes a get request to the specified URL. The request headers and other options can be configured using the second argument.
- `post(url: string, options?: RequestOptionsArgs)`: This makes a post request to the specified URL. The request body, headers, and other options can be configured using the second argument.
- `put(url: string, options?: RequestOptionsArgs)`: This makes a put request to the specified URL. The request headers and other options can be configured using the second argument.
- `patch(url: string, options?: RequestOptionsArgs)`: This makes a patch request to the specified URL. The request headers and other options can be configured using the second argument.
- `delete(url: string, options?: RequestOptionsArgs)`: This makes a delete request to the specified URL. The request headers and other options can be configured using the second argument.
- `head(url: string, options?: RequestOptionsArgs)`: This makes a head request to the specified URL. The request headers and other options can be configured using the second argument.

Using Angular's HTTP module

Now, let's implement the logic for importing the existing developers from GitHub. First, we will need to import the `HttpModule` in our `AppModule`:

```
import {HttpModule} from '@angular/http';
...
```

```
@NgModule({
  imports: [..., HttpModule],
  declarations: [...],
  providers: [...],
  bootstrap: [...]
})
class AppModule {}
...
```

After that, open the ch6/ts/step-2/add_developer.ts file and enter the following imports:

```
import {Response} from '@angular/http';
import {GitHubGateway} from './github_gateway';
```

Add GitHubGateway to the list of providers of the AddDeveloper component:

```
@Component({
  ...
  providers: [GitHubGateway]
})
class AddDeveloper {...}
```

As the next step, we have to include the following parameters in the constructor of the class:

```
constructor(private githubAPI: GitHubGateway,
  private developers: DeveloperCollection,
  fb: FormBuilder) {
  //...
}
```

This way, the AddDeveloper class' instances will have a private property called githubAPI.

The only thing left is to implement the addDeveloper method and allow the user to import the existing developers using the GitHubGateway instance.

Once the user presses the **Add** button, we will need to check whether we need to import an existing GitHub user or add a new developer. For this purpose, we can use the value of the fetchFromGitHub control:

```
if (this.importDevForm.controls['fetchFromGitHub'].value) {
  // Import developer
} else {
  // Add new developer
}
```

If it has a truthy value, then we can invoke the `getUser` method of the `githubAPI` property and pass the value of the `githubHandle` control as an argument:

```
this.githubAPI.getUser(model.githubHandle)
```

In the `getUser` method of the `GitHubGateway` instance, we delegate the call to the `Http` service's `get` method, which returns an observable. In order to get the result that the observable will push, we will need to pass a callback to its `subscribe` method:

```
this.githubAPI.getUser(model.githubHandle)
  .map((r: Response) => r.json())
  .subscribe((res: any) => {
    // "res" contains the response of the GitHub's API
  });
```

In the preceding snippet, we first establish the HTTP `get` request. After this, we get the corresponding observable that, in general cases, will emit a series of values (in this case, only a single one–the response of the request) and map them to their JSON representations. If the request fails, or the response's body is not a valid JSON string, then we will get an error.

 Note that, in order to reduce the bundle size of Angular, the team at Google has included only the core of RxJS in the framework. In order to use the `map` and `catch` methods, you will need to add the following imports at `add_developer.ts`:
```
import 'rxjs/add/operator/map';
import 'rxjs/add/operator/catch';
```

Now, let's implement the body of the callback we pass to `subscribe`:

```
let dev = new Developer();
dev.githubHandle = res.login;
dev.email = res.email;
dev.popular = res.followers >= 1000;
dev.realName = res.name;
dev.id = res.id;
dev.avatarUrl = res.avatar_url;
this.developers.addDeveloper(dev);
this.successMessage = `Developer ${dev.githubHandle} successfully imported
from GitHub`;
```

In the preceding example, we set the properties of a new `Developer` instance. Here, we establish the mapping between the object returned from GitHub's API and the developer's representation in our application. We consider a developer as popular if they have more than 1,000 followers.

The entire implementation of the `addDeveloper` method can be found at `ch7/ts/multi-page-model-driven/add_developer.ts`.

> In order to handle failed requests, we can use the `catch` method of the observable instances:
> ```
> this.githubAPI.getUser(model.githubHandle)
> .catch((error, source, caught) => {
>   console.log(error)
>   return error;
> });
> ```

Defining parameterized views

As the next step, let's dedicate a special page for each developer. On it, we'll be able to take a detailed look at their profile. Once the user clicks on the name of any of the developers on the home page of the application, they should be redirected to a page with a detailed profile of the selected developer. The end result will look as follows:

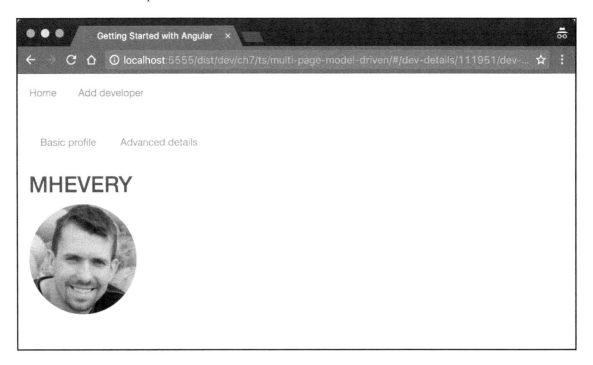

Figure 2

In order to do this, we will need to pass an identifier of the developer to the component that shows the developer's detailed profile. Open `app.ts`, and add the following import:

```
import {DeveloperDetails} from './developer_details';
```

We haven't developed the `DeveloperDetails` component yet, so, if you run the application, you will get an error. We will define the component in the next paragraph, but before this, let's alter the routes' definition of the `app.ts`:

```
const routingModule = RouterModule.forRoot([
  ...
  {
    component: DeveloperDetails,
    path: 'dev-details/:id',
    children: devDetailsRoutes
  }
]);
```

We add a single route with the `dev-details/:id` path and associate the `DeveloperDetails` component with it.

Note that, in the `path` property, we declare that the route has a single parameter called `id` and also set the `children` property to the `devDetailsRoutes`. The `devDetailsRoutes` contains the nested routes, which should be rendered within the `router-outlet` located in `DeveloperDetails` component.

Now, let's pass the `id` of the current developer as a parameter to the `routerLink` directive. Open `home.html` in your working directory and replace the table cell, where we display the developer's `realName` property with the following content:

```
<td>
  <a [routerLink]="['/dev-details', dev.id, 'dev-basic-info']">
    {{dev.realName}}
  </a>
</td>
```

The value of the `routerLink` directive is an array with the following three elements:

- `'/dev-details'`: A string that shows the root route.
- `dev.id`: The ID of the developer whose details we want to see.
- `'dev-basic-info'`: The path of a route that shows which component within the nested route should be rendered.

Defining nested routes

Now, let's jump to the `DeveloperDetails` definition. In your working directory, create a file called `developer_details.ts` and enter the following content:

```
import {Component} from '@angular/core';
import {ActivatedRoute} from '@angular/router';
import {Developer} from './developer';
import {DeveloperCollection} from './developer_collection';
import {DeveloperBasicInfo} from './developer_basic_info';
import {DeveloperAdvancedInfo} from './developer_advanced_info';

import 'rxjs/add/operator/take';

@Component({
  selector: 'dev-details',
  template: `...`,
})
export class DeveloperDetails {
  public dev: Developer;

  constructor(private route: ActivatedRoute,
    private developers: DeveloperCollection) {}

  ngOnInit() {
    this.route.params.take(1)
      .subscribe((params: any) => {
        this.dev = this.developers.getUserById(parseInt(params['id']));
      });
  }
}

export const devDetailsRoutes = [...];
```

 For the sake of simplicity, in order to not introduce a complex directory/file structure in the examples for this book, we have a few component and route declarations in a single file. Keep in mind that, according to best practices, the individual declarations should be placed into separate files. For further information, visit `https://angular.io/styleguide`.

In the previous snippet, we define a component with controller called `DeveloperDetails`. Note that, within the controller's constructor, through the DI mechanism of Angular, we inject a parameter associated with the `ActivatedRoute` token. The injected parameter provides us with access to the parameters visible by the current route. In `ngOnInit`, we apply an imperative approach, where we subscribe changes in the value of the route's `params` property, get the first set of parameters, and assign the `dev` property to the result of the invocation of `this.developers.getUserById` with the selected developer's identifier as an argument.

> Note that a more declarative and reactive approach would be to take advantage of the higher-order functions provided by RxJS, where we'd be able to get access to the selected developer using code similar to the following:
>
> ```
> ...
> get dev$() {
>   return this.route.params.map((params: any) =>
>     this.developers.getUserById(parseInt(params['id'])));
> }
> ...
> ```
>
> Later, we can bind to the result of the invocation with the Angular's async pipe, that we will explain later in this chapter.

Since the parameter we got from `routeParams.params['id']` is a string, we will need to parse it to a number in order to get the developer associated with the given route.

Now, let's define the child routes, which will be rendered in the template of `DeveloperDetails`:

```
export const devDetailsRoutes = [
  { path: '', redirectTo: 'dev-basic-info', pathMatch: 'full' },
  { component: DeveloperBasicInfo, path: 'dev-basic-info' },
  { component: DeveloperAdvancedInfo, path: 'dev-details-advanced' }
];
```

In the preceding code, there is nothing new for us. The route definition follows the exact same rules we're already familiar with.

Now, to the template of the component, let's add links associated with the individual nested routes:

```
@Component({
  selector: 'dev-details',
  template: `
    <section class="col-md-4">
    <ul class="nav nav-tabs">
      <li><a [routerLink]="['./dev-basic-info']">Basic profile</a></li>
      <li><a [routerLink]="['./dev-details-advanced']">Advanced
details</a></li>
```

```
      </ul>
      <router-outlet></router-outlet>
      </section>
      `
})
export class DeveloperDetails {...}
```

Within the template, we declare two relative to the current path links. The first one points to `dev-basic-info`, which is the path of the first route defined within `devDetailsRoutes`, and the second one points to `dev-details-advanced`.

Since the implementations of the components associated with both routes are quite similar, let's take a look only at `DeveloperBasicInfo`. As an exercise, you can develop the second one or take a look at its implementation at `ch7/ts/multi-page-model-driven/developer_advanced_info.ts`:

```
import {Component, Inject, forwardRef, Host} from '@angular/core';
import {DeveloperDetails} from './developer_details';
import {Developer} from './developer';

@Component({
  selector: 'dev-details-basic',
  styles: [`
    .avatar {
      border-radius: 150px;
    }`
  ],
  template: `
    <h2>{{dev.githubHandle | uppercase}}</h2>
    <img *ngIf="dev.avatarUrl == null" class="avatar"
src="http://hippycanada.ca/wordpress/wp-content/uploads/2014/12/gravatar-60
-grey.jpg" width="150">
    <img *ngIf="dev.avatarUrl != null" class="avatar" [src]="dev.avatarUrl"
width="150">
    `
})
export class DeveloperBasicInfo {
  dev: Developer;

  constructor(@Inject(forwardRef(() => DeveloperDetails))
    @Host() parent: DeveloperDetails) {
   this.dev = parent.dev;
  }
}
```

In the preceding snippet, we inject the parent component using the `@Inject` parameter decorator. Inside `@Inject`, we use `forwardRef`, since we have a circular dependency between the `developer_basic_info` and `developer_details` packages (inside `developer_basic_info`, we import `developer_details`, and within `developer_details`, we import `developer_basic_info`).

We need a reference to the instance of the parent component in order to get the instance of the current developer that corresponds to the selected route.

Transforming data with pipes

It is time to take a look at the last building block that Angular provides for the development of applications that we haven't covered in detail yet–the pipes.

Just like the filters in AngularJS, pipes are intended to encapsulate all the data transformation logic. Let's take a look at the template of the home page of the application we have just developed:

```
...
<td [ngSwitch]="dev.popular">
  <span *ngSwitchCase="true">Yes</span>
  <span *ngSwitchCase="false">Not yet</span>
</td>
...
```

In the preceding snippet, depending on the value of the `popular` property, we show different data using the `NgSwitch` and `NgSwitchCase` directives. Although this works, it is redundant.

Developing stateless pipes

Let's develop a pipe that transforms the value of the `popular` property and uses it in place of `NgSwitch` and `NgSwitchCase`. The pipe will accept three arguments: a value that should be transformed, a string that should be displayed when the value is truthy, and another string that should be displayed in case of a falsy value.

With the use of an Angular custom pipe, we will be able to simplify the template to the following:

```
<td>{{dev.popular | boolean: 'Yes': 'No'}}</td>
```

We could even use emojis, as follows:

```
<td>{{dev.popular | boolean: '👍': '👎'}}</td>
```

We apply the pipe to the value the same way we would do in AngularJS. The arguments we pass to the pipe should be separated by the colon (:) symbol.

In order to develop an Angular pipe, we will need the following imports:

```
import {Pipe, PipeTransform} from '@angular/core';
```

The `Pipe` decorator can be used for adding metadata to the class that implements the data transformation logic. The `PipeTransform` is an interface with a single method, called `transform`:

```
import {Pipe, PipeTransform} from '@angular/core';

@Pipe({ name: 'boolean' })
export class BooleanPipe implements PipeTransform {
  transform(flag: boolean, trueValue: any, falseValue: any): string {
    return flag ? trueValue : falseValue;
  }
}
```

The preceding snippet is the entire implementation of `BooleanPipe`. The `name` that we pass to the `@Pipe` decorator determines how we should reference it in templates.

The last thing we need to do before being able to use the `BooleanPipe` is to add it to the list of declarations in our `AppModule`:

```
@NgModule({
  ...
  declarations: [..., BooleanPipe, ...],
  ...
})
class AppModule {}
```

Using Angular's built-in pipes

Angular provides the following set of built-in pipes:

- `CurrencyPipe`: This pipe is used for formatting currency data. As an argument, it accepts the abbreviation of the currency type (that is, `"EUR"`, `"USD"`, and so on). It can be used in the following way:

  ```
  {{ currencyValue | currency: 'USD' }} <!-- USD42 -->
  ```

- `DatePipe`: This pipe is used for the transformation of dates. It can be used in the following way:

  ```
  {{ dateValue | date: 'shortTime'  }} <!-- 12:00 AM -->
  ```

- `DecimalPipe`: This pipe is used for transformation of decimal numbers. The argument it accepts is of the following form: `"{minIntegerDigits}.{minFractionDigits}-{maxFractionDigits}"`. It can be used in the following way:

  ```
  {{ 42.1618 | number: '3.1-2' }} <!-- 042.16 -->
  ```

- `JsonPipe`: This transforms a JavaScript object into a JSON string. It can be used in the following way:

  ```
  {{ { foo: 42 } | json }} <!-- { "foo": 42 } -->
  ```

- `LowerCasePipe`: This transforms a string to lowercase. It can be used in the following way:

  ```
  {{ FOO | lowercase }} <!-- foo -->
  ```

- `UpperCasePipe`: This transforms a string to uppercase. It can be used in the following way:

  ```
  {{ 'foo' | uppercase }} <!-- FOO -->
  ```

- `PercentPipe`: This transforms a number into a percentage. It can be used in the following way:

  ```
  {{ 42 | percent: '2.1-2' }}  <!-- 4,200.0% -->
  ```

- `SlicePipe`: This returns a slice of an array. The pipe accepts the start and the end indexes of the slice. It can be used in the following way:

  ```
  {{ [1, 2, 3] | slice: 1: 2 }} <!-- 2 -->
  ```

- `AsyncPipe`: This is a `stateful` pipe that accepts an observable or a promise; we will take a look at it at the end of the chapter.

Developing stateful pipes

There is one common thing among all the pipes mentioned earlier — all of them return exactly the same result each time we apply them to the same value and pass them the same set of arguments. Such pipes, which hold the referentially transparency property, are called **pure pipes**.

The `@Pipe` decorator accepts an object literal of the `{ name: string, pure?: boolean }` type, where the default value for the `pure` property is `true`. This means that, when we define any given pipe, we can declare whether it is stateful or stateless. The pure property is important because, in case the pipe is stateless (that is, it returns the same result in case it is applied over the same value with the same set of arguments), the change detection can be optimized.

Now, let's build a stateful pipe. Our pipe will make an HTTP `get` request to a JSON API. For this purpose, we will use the `@angular/http` module.

 Note that having business logic in a pipe is not considered as a best practice. This type of logic should be extracted into a service. The example here is for learning purposes only.

In this case, the pipe needs to hold a different state depending on the status of the request (that is, whether it is pending or completed). We will use the pipe in the following way:

```
{{ "http://example.com/user.json" | fetchJson | json }}
```

This way, we apply the `fetchJson` pipe over the URL. Once we have the body of the response, we can apply the `json` pipe over it. This example also shows how we can chain pipes with Angular.

Similar to stateless pipes, for the development of stateful pipes, we have to decorate the class that implements the pipe's logic with @Pipe and implement the PipeTransform interface. This time, because of the HTTP request functionality, we will also need to import the Http and Response classes from the @angular/http module:

```
import {Pipe, PipeTransform} from '@angular/core';
import {Http, Response} from '@angular/http';
import 'rxjs/add/operator/toPromise';
```

Each time it happens to apply the fetchJson pipe to an argument with a different value, we will need to make a new HTTP get request. This means that, as the state of the pipe, we need to keep at least the values of the response of the remote service and the last URL:

```
@Pipe({
  name: 'fetchJson',
  pure: false
})
export class FetchJsonPipe implements PipeTransform {
  private data: any;
  private prevUrl: string = null;
  constructor(private http: Http) {}
  transform(url: string): any {...}
}
```

The only piece of logic we need to implement is the transform method:

```
...
transform(url: string): any {
  if (this.prevUrl !== url) {
    this.http.get(url).toPromise(Promise)
      .then((data: Response) => data.json())
      .then(result => this.data = result);
    this.prevUrl = url;
  }
  return this.data || {};
}
...
```

Inside of it, we initially compare the URL passed as an argument with the one we already have (by default, it's value will be null). If they are different, we initiate a new HTTP get request using the local instance of the Http class, which was passed to the constructor function. Once the request is completed, we parse the response to JSON and set the data property to the result.

Now, let's suppose that the pipe has started an `Http get` request, and before it is completed, the change detection mechanism invokes the pipe again. In this case, we will compare the `prevUrl` property with the `url` parameter. If they are the same, we won't perform a new `http` request and will immediately return the value of the `data` property. If `prevUrl` has a different value from `url`, we will start a new request.

Using stateful pipes

Now, let's use the pipe that we developed. The application that we will implement provides a text input and a button with label **Get Avatar** to the user. Once the user enters a value in the text input and presses the button, the avatar corresponding to the GitHub user will appear below the text input, as shown in the following screenshot:

Figure 3

Now, let's develop a sample component, which will allow us to enter the GitHub user's handle:

```
// ch7/ts/statful_pipe/app.ts

@Component({
  selector: 'app',
  template: `
    <input type="text" #input>
    <button (click)="setUsername(input.value)">Get Avatar</button>
```

```
})
class App {
  username: string;
  setUsername(user: string) {
    this.username = user;
  }
}
```

The only thing left is to show the GitHub avatar of the user. We can easily achieve this by altering the template of the preceding component with the following img declaration:

```
<img width="160"
  [src]="(('https://api.github.com/users/' + username) |
fetchJson).avatar_url">
```

Initially, we append the GitHub handle to the base URL used for fetching users from the API. Later, we will apply the fetchJson filter over it and get the avatar_url property from the returned result.

Using Angular's AsyncPipe

Angular's AsyncPipe transform method accepts an observable or a promise as an argument. Once the argument pushes a value (that is, the promise has been resolved or the subscribe callback of the observable is invoked), AsyncPipe will return it as a result. Let's take a look at the following example:

```
// ch7/ts/async-pipe/app.ts

@Component({
  selector: 'greeting',
  template: 'Hello {{ greetingPromise | async }}'
})
class Greeting {
  greetingPromise = new Promise<string>(resolve => this.resolve = resolve);
  resolve: Function;

  constructor() {
    setTimeout(_ => {
      this.resolve('Foobar!');
    }, 3000);
  }
}
```

Here, we define an Angular component that has two properties, that is, `greetingPromise` of the type `Promise<string>` and `resolve` of the type `Function`. We initialized the `greetingPromise` property with a new `Promise<string>` instance, and as the value of the `resolve` property, we set the `resolve` callback of the `promise`.

In the constructor of the class, we start a time-out with the duration of 3,000 ms, and inside of its callback, we resolve the promise. Once the promise is resolved, the value of the expression `{{ greetingPromise | async }}` will be evaluated to the string `Foobar!`. The end result that the user will see on the screen is the text **"Hello Foobar!"**.

The `async` pipe is extremely powerful when we combine it with an `Http` request or with an observable, which pushes a sequence of values.

Using AsyncPipe with observables

We're already familiar with the concept of observables from the previous chapters. We can say that an observable object allows us to subscribe to the emission of a sequence of values, for instance:

```
let observer = Observable.create(observer => {
  setInterval(() => {
    observer.next(new Date().getTime());
  }, 1000);
});
observer.subscribe(date => console.log(date));
```

Once we subscribe to the observable, it will start emitting values each second, which will be printed in the console. Let's combine this snippet with component definition and implement a simple timer:

```
// ch7/ts/async-pipe/app.ts

@Component({  selector: 'timer' })
class Timer {
  username: string;
  timer: Observable<number>;

  constructor() {
    let counter = 0;
    this.timer = new Observable<number>(observer => {
      setInterval(() => {
        observer.next(new Date().getTime());
      }, 1000);
    });
  }
```

```
    }
```

The only thing left in order to be able to use the timer component is to add its template. We can subscribe to the observable directly in the template using the `async` pipe:

```
{{ timer | async | date: "medium" }}
```

This way, each second we will get the new value emitted by the observable, and the `date` pipe will transform it into a readable form.

Summary

In this chapter, we took a deep dive into the Angular's forms module, by developing a model-driven (reactive) form and combining it with the HTTP module. We took a look at some advanced features of the new component-based router and saw how we can use and develop custom stateful and stateless pipes.

The next chapter will be dedicated to how we can make our Angular applications SEO-friendly by taking advantage of the server-side rendering that the module Universal provides. Another thing that we'll take a look at is angular-cli and other tools that make our experience as developers better. Finally, we'll explain what Ahead-of-Time compilation is in the context of Angular, and why we should take advantage of it in our applications.declarations should be placed into separate files. For further information,

8

Tooling and Development Experience

We are already familiar with all the core concepts of Angular. We know how to develop a component-based user interface, taking advantage of all the building blocks that the framework provides — directives, components, dependency injections, pipes, forms, and the brand new router.

For the final step, we'll look at where to begin when we want to build a **single-page application** (**SPA**) from scratch. This chapter describes how to do the following:

- Use Web Workers for performance-sensitive applications.
- Build SEO-friendly applications with server-side rendering.
- Bootstrap a project as quickly as possible.
- Enhance our experience as developers.
- What is **Ahead-of-Time** (**AoT**) compilation and how to use it.

So, let's begin!

Running an application in a Web Worker

When talking about performance in the context of frontend Web development, we can either mean network, computational, or rendering performance. In this section, we'll concentrate on rendering and computational performance, which are very tightly related.

First, let's draw parallels between a Web application and a video file, and between a browser and a video player. The biggest difference between the Web application running in the browser and the video file playing in the video player is that the web page needs to be generated dynamically, in contrast to the video which has been recorded, encoded, and distributed. However, in both cases, the user of the application sees a sequence of frames; the core difference is in how these frames are generated. In the world of video processing, when we play a video, we have it already recorded; it is the responsibility of the video decoder to extract the individual frames based on the compression algorithm. In contrast to this, on the Web, JavaScript, HTML, and CSS are in charge of producing frames that are rendered later by the browser's rendering engine.

In the context of the browser, we can think of each frame as a snapshot of the web page at a given moment. The different frames are rendered fast, one after the other; so, in theory, the end user of the application should see them smoothly incorporated together, just like a video played in a video player.

On the Web, we try to reach 60 fps (frames per second), which means that each frame has about 16 milliseconds to be computed and rendered on the screen. This duration includes the time required by the browser to make all the necessary calculations for the layout and the rendering of the page (the browser's internal computations), and the time that our JavaScript needs to execute.

In the end, we have less than 16 milliseconds (because of the browser's internal computations) for our JavaScript to finish its execution. If it doesn't fit in this duration, the frame rate will drop by half. Since JavaScript is a single-threaded language, all the calculations need to happen in the main UI thread, which can lead to a very poor user experience because of the frame drop.

HTML5 introduced an API called **Web Workers**, which allows the execution of client-side code into multiple threads. For the sake of simplicity, the standard doesn't allow shared memory between individual threads, but instead allows communication with message passing. The messages exchanged between Web Workers and the main UI thread must be strings, which often require the serialization and deserialization of JSON strings.

The lack of shared memory between the individual workers, and the workers and the main UI thread brings a couple of limitations, some of which are as follows:

- Disabled access to the DOM by the worker threads.
- Global variables cannot be shared among the individual computational units (that is, worker threads and main UI threads and vice versa).

Web Workers and Angular

On account of the platform agnostic design of Angular, the core team decided to take advantage of this API; during the summer of 2015, Google embedded Web Workers support into the framework. This feature allows most of the Angular applications to be run on a separate thread, making the main UI thread responsible only for rendering. This helps us achieve the goal of 60 fps much more easily than running the entire application in a single thread.

Web Workers support is not enabled by default. When enabling it, we need to keep something in mind–in a Web Worker-ready application, the components will not be run in the main UI thread, which does not allow us to directly manipulate the DOM. In this case, we need to use APIs on a higher-level of abstraction, provided by Angular, for establishing data binding or manipulating the elements' properties.

Bootstrapping an application running in a Web Worker

Let's make the to-do application that we developed in `Chapter 4`, *Getting Started with Angular Components and Directives* work in a Web Worker. You can find the example that we'll explore at `ch8/ts/todo_webworkers/`.

 Note that the Web Worker module is not finalized yet, so its API may change in future versions of Angular. On the other hand, the conceptual idea and the architecture are mature enough, so most likely there will not be any fundamental differences.

First of all, let's discuss the changes that we will need to make. Take a look at `ch4/ts/inputs-outputs/app.ts`. Note that, inside `app.ts`, we include the `platformBrowserDynamic` function from the `@angular/platform-browser-dynamic` module. This is the first thing we need to modify. The bootstrap process of an application running in a background process is different.

Before refactoring our code, let's take a look at a diagram that illustrates the bootstrap process of a typical Angular application running in Web Workers:

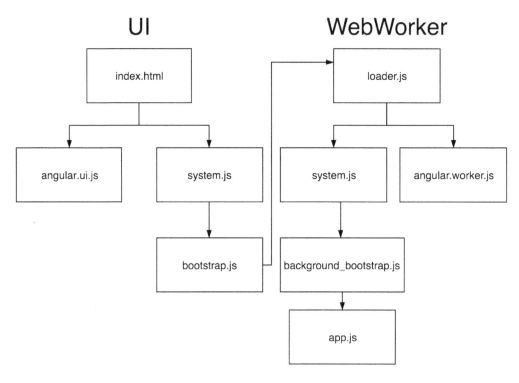

Figure 1

This diagram has two parts: **UI** and **WebWorker**. **UI** shows the actions performed during initialization in the main UI thread; the **WebWorker** part of the diagram shows how the application is bootstrapped in the background thread. Now, let's explain the bootstrap process step-by-step.

First, the user opens the `index.html` page, which triggers the download of the following two files:

- The UI bundle of Angular used for applications running in Web Worker.
- The `system.js` bundle (we talked about the global object `System` in Chapter 3, *TypeScript Crash Course*. We can think of the `system.js` bundle as a polyfill for the module loader).

Using `system.js`, we download the script used for the initialization of the part of the application running in the main UI thread (`bootstrap.js`). This script starts `loader.js` in Web Worker. This is the first script that runs in a background thread. Once the worker is started, `loader.js` will download `system.js` and the bundle of Angular, which is meant to be run in the background thread. The first request will usually hit the cache because `system.js` is already requested by the main thread. Using the module loader, we download the script that is responsible for bootstrapping the background app `background_bootstrap.js`, which will finally start the functionality of our application, in Web Worker.

From now on, the entire application that we built will be run in Web Worker and will exchange messages with the main UI thread to respond to user events and render instructions.

Now that we are aware of the basic flow of events during initialization when using workers, let's refactor our to-do application to take advantage of them.

Migrating an application to Web Worker

Let's show how we can make an application compatible with Web Workers. This way, we can reduce the frame drop in computationally intensive apps, since we'll free the main UI thread and let it be responsible only for rendering.

Inside `index.html`, we will need to add the following scripts:

```
<!-- ch8/ts/todo_webworkers/index.html -->
...
<script src="/node_modules/systemjs/dist/system.src.js">
</script>
<script src="/node_modules/reflect-metadata/Reflect.js"></script>
<script src="/node_modules/zone.js/dist/zone.js">
</script>
<!-
   Contains some basic SystemJS configuration in order to
   allow us to load Angular
-->
<script src="./config.js"></script>
<script>
System.import('./bootstrap.js')
   .catch(function () {
     console.log('Report this error to
https://github.com/mgechev/getting-started-with-angular/issues', e);
   });
</script>
```

. . .

In the preceding snippet, we've included references to `system.js`, `zone.js`, and `reflect-metadata`. `zone.js` is a polyfill for the zones that Angular exclusively uses, that we mentioned earlier in the book. `reflect-metadata` contains another polyfill for the Metadata Reflection API, which at the moment of writing is not yet available in browsers.

For the next step, we will explicitly import the `bootstrap.js` file, which contains the logic used to start the `loader.js` script in Web Worker.

Let's explore `bootstrap.ts`, which is the original TypeScript version of the transpiled `bootstrap.js`:

```
// ch8/ts/todo_webworkers/bootstrap.ts

//main entry point
import {bootstrapWorkerUi} from '@angular/platform-webworker';

bootstrapWorkerUi('loader.js');
```

We pass `'loader.js'` to the invocation of `bootstrapWorkerUi`. This way, Angular knows that `loader.js` will run in a background thread. The script is located in the application's root.

Now, we can move to the right-hand side of the diagram shown in the *Bootstrapping an application running in a Web Worker* section. The logic in `loader.ts` (the original TypeScript version of `loader.js`) is quite simple:

```
// ch8/ts/todo_webworkers/loader.ts

importScripts('/node_modules/systemjs/dist/system.src.js',
       '/node_modules/reflect-metadata/Reflect.js',
       '/node_modules/zone.js/dist/zone.js',
       './config.js');

System.import('./background_app.js')
.then(() => console.log('The application has started successfully'),
  error => console.error('error loading background', error));
```

As the first step, we import `SystemJS`, `ReflectMetadata` polyfils, `zone.js`, and the configuration for `SystemJS`. As this script is already run in Web Workers, we have the `importScripts` function, which allows us to load the listed files synchronously. As the last step, with `System`, we import the script that contains our application.

Now, let's explore how we bootstrap the application inside of the Web Worker:

```
// ch8/ts/todo_webworkers/background_app.ts

import {platformWorkerAppDynamic}
  from '@angular/platform-webworker-dynamic';

// Logic for the application...

platformWorkerAppDynamic().bootstrapModule(AppModule)
  .catch(err => console.error(err));
```

The preceding process is quite similar to what we used to do when bootstrapping an Angular application running in the main UI thread. We import the `platformWorkerAppDynamic` function and invoke it with the root module of the application as its first argument.

Making an application compatible with Web Workers

As we said, the code that runs in the context of Web Worker does not have access to the DOM. Let's see what changes we need to make in order to address this limitation.

This is the original implementation of the `InputBox` component:

```
// ch4/ts/inputs-outputs/app.ts

@Component({
  selector: 'input-box',
  template: `
    <input #todoInput [placeholder]="inputPlaceholder">
    <button (click)="emitText(todoInput.value);
      todoInput.value = '';">
      {{buttonLabel}}
    </button>
  `
})
class InputBox {
  @Input() inputPlaceholder: string;
  @Input() buttonLabel: string;
  @Output() inputText = new EventEmitter<string>();

  emitText(text: string) {
    this.inputText.emit(text);
  }
```

```
    }
```

Note that, inside the template, we reference the input element with the identifier `todoInput` and use the reference within the expression set as the handler of the click event. This code will not be able to run in Web Worker, since we directly access a DOM element inside the template. In order to take care of this, we will need to refactor the snippet, so it uses Angular data binding instead of directly touching any element. We can either use inputs when a single direction binding makes sense or `NgModel` to achieve two-way data binding, which is a bit more computationally intensive.

Let's use `NgModel`:

```
// ch8/ts/todo_webworkers/background_app.ts
import {NgModel} from '@angular/common';

@Component({
  selector: 'input-box',
  template: `
    <input [placeholder]="inputPlaceholder" [(ngModel)]="input">
    <button (click)="emitText()">
      {{buttonLabel}}
    </button>
  `
})
class InputBox {
  @Input() inputPlaceholder: string;
  @Input() buttonLabel: string;
  @Output() inputText = new EventEmitter<string>();
  input: string;

  emitText() {
    this.inputText.emit(this.input);
    this.input = '';
  }
}
```

In this version of the `InputBox` component, we create a two-way data binding between the input element and the `input` property of the `InputBox` component. Once the user clicks on the button, the `emitText` method will be invoked, which will trigger a new event emitted by `inputText EventEmitter`. In order to reset the value of the input element, we take advantage of the two-way data binding mechanism of Angular and set the value of the `input` property to the empty string; this will automatically update the UI.

Moving the entire logic from the templates of the components to their controllers brings a lot of benefits, such as improved testability, maintainability, code reuse, and clarity.

The preceding code is compatible with the Web Worker environment, as the `NgModel` directive is based on an abstraction that does not manipulate the DOM directly. Instead, it delegates this responsibility to another abstraction called `Renderer`, which when running in a Web Worker exchanges messages asynchronously with the main UI thread.

To recap, we can say that, while running applications in the context of Web Workers, we need to keep the following two things in mind:

- We need to use a different bootstrap process.
- We should not access the DOM directly.

Typical scenarios that violate the second point are as follows:

- Changing the DOM of the page by selecting an element and manipulating it directly with the browser's native APIs or with a third-party library.
- Accessing native elements injected using `ElementRef`.
- Creating a reference to an element in the template and passing it as an argument to methods.
- Directly manipulating an element referenced within the template.

In all these scenarios, we would need to use the higher-level APIs provided by Angular. If we build our applications according to this practice, we will benefit not only from being able to run them in Web Workers, but also from increasing the code reuse in case we want to use them across different platforms.

Keeping this in mind and following best practices will also allow us to take advantage of server-side rendering.

Initial load of a SPA

In this section, we will explore what a server-side rendering is, why we need it in our applications, and how we can use it with Angular.

For our purpose, we'll explain the typical flow of events when a user opens a SPA implemented in Angular. First, we'll trace the events with the server-side rendering disabled, and after that, we'll see how we can benefit from this feature by enabling it. Our example will be illustrated in the context of HTTP 1.1:

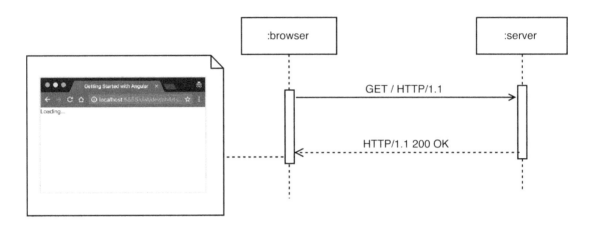

Figure 2

Figure 2 shows the first request by the browser and the corresponding server's response when loading a typical SPA. The result that the client will see initially is the content of the HTML page without any rendered components.

Let's suppose that we deploy the to-do application we built in Chapter 4, *Getting Started with Angular Components and Directives*, to a web server that has the example.com domain associated with it.

Once the user navigates to https://example.com/, the browser will open a new HTTP GET request, fetching the root resource (/). When the server receives the request, it will respond with an HTML file that, in our case, will look something like this:

```
<!DOCTYPE html>
<html lang="en">
<head>
  <title>...</title>
  <link rel="stylesheet" href="bootstrap.min.css">
</head>
<body>
  <app>Loading...</app>
  <script src="es6-shim.min.js"></script>
  <script src="Reflect.js"></script>
  <script src="system.src.js"></script>
  <script src="angular-polyfills.js"></script>
  <script src="Rx.min.js"></script>
  <script src="angular.js"></script>
```

```
    <script src="router.js"></script>
    <script src="http.min.js"></script>
    <script>...</script>
  </body>
</html>
```

The browser will receive this content as the body of the response. When the markup is rendered onto the screen, all that the user will see is the **Loading...** label.

In the next step, the browser will find all the references in the HTML file's external resources, such as styles and scripts, and start to download them. In our case, some of them are `bootstrap.css`, `es6-shim.min.js`, `Reflect.js`, `system.src.js`, and `angular-polyfills.js`.

Once all the referenced resources are available, there still won't be any significant visual progress for the user (except if the styles from the downloaded CSS file are applied to the page). This won't change until the JavaScript virtual machine processes all the referenced scripts related to the application's implementation. At this point, Angular will know which component needs to be rendered based on the current URL and configuration.

If the component associated with the page is defined in a separate file outside of our main application bundle, the framework will need to download it together with its entire dependency graph.

If we're using JiT compilation, in case the template and the styles of the component are externalized, Angular will need to download them as well before it is able to render the requested page. Right after this, the framework will be able to compile the template associated with the target component and render the page.

In this scenario, these are the two main pitfalls:

- In case of large applications and/or poor Internet connection, the user experience will be poor.
- Search engines are not that good at indexing dynamic content generated by JavaScript; this means that the **SEO** (**Search Engine Optimization**) of our SPA will suffer.

In the past, we solved the SEO issue in the applications built with AngularJS with different workarounds, such as using a headless browser for rendering the requested page, caching it onto the disk, and later providing it to search engines. However, there's a more elegant solution.

Initial load of a SPA with server-side rendering

A couple of years ago, libraries such as *Rendr, Derby, Meteor,* and the others introduced the concept of **isomorphic** JavaScript applications, which were later renamed **universal**. In essence, universal applications could be run both on the client and on the server. Such portability is only possible in the case of low coupling between the SPA and the browser's APIs. The greatest benefit of this paradigm is that the application can be rendered on the server and sent to the client.

Universal applications are not framework specific; we can take advantage of them in any framework that can be run outside of the environment of the browser. Conceptually, the practice of server-side rendering is very similar across platforms and libraries; only its implementation details may differ. For instance, the Angular Universal module, which implements server-side rendering, supports node.js as well as ASP.NET.

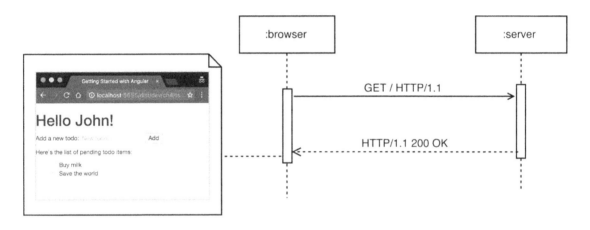

Figure 3

Figure 3 shows the response by the server to the initial browser GET request. This time, in contrast to the typical scenario of loading a SPA, the browser will receive the HTML of the rendered page.

Let's trace the flow of the events in the same application with the server-side rendering feature enabled. In this case, once the server receives the HTTP GET request by the browser, it will run the SPA on the server in the environment of node.js. All the DOM calls will be redirected to a server-side DOM implementation and executed in the context of the used platform. Similarly, all the AJAX calls with the Angular HTTP module will be handled by the server-side implementation of the module. This way, the application will not make any difference, whether it is running in the context of the browser or the server.

Once the rendered version of the SPA is available, it can be serialized to HTML and sent to the browser. This time, during the application's initialization, instead of the **Loading...** label, the user will see the page they requested right away.

Note that, at this point, the client will have the rendered version of the application, but all the referenced external resources, such as scripts and styles, still need to be available. This means that, initially, none of the CSS styles declared in the external files will be applied and the application will not be responsive to any user-related interactions, such as the mouse and keyboard events.

Note that in case the scripts are inlined on the server-side rendered page, the application will be responsive to user events. However, inlining big chunks of JavaScript is generally considered a bad practice, as it will increase the page's size dramatically and prevent the scripts from caching; both will influence the network performance.

When the JavaScript virtual machine processes the JavaScript associated with the page, our SPA will be ready to use.

Server-side rendering with Angular

During the first half of 2015, Patrick Stapleton and Jeff Whelpley announced that they had started the development of the module, **Universal**. Universal is a library that allows us to build universal (also called isomorphic) JavaScript applications with Angular; in other words, it provides server-side rendering support.

Applications using Angular Universal and rendered on the server will not be responsive to user interaction until all the JavaScript belonging to the requested page has been processed. This is a drawback that we already mentioned, which is valid for all server-side rendered applications. To handle this problem, Patrick and Jeff introduced **preboot.js**, which is a lightweight library that will be inlined on the page rendered by the server and available after the initial client request.

Preboot.js has several strategies for the management of the received client events before the application is completely initialized; they are as follows:

- Recording and playing back events.
- Responding immediately to events.
- Maintaining focus when a page is re-rendered.
- Buffering client-side re-rendering for smoother transition.
- Freezing a page until the bootstrap is complete if a user clicks on a button.

At the time of writing this book, the Universal module was still being actively developed. You can give it a try using the Angular universal starter at `https://github.com/angular/universal-starter`.

Enhancing our development experience

Our experience as developers can be enhanced in terms of productivity or by allowing us to have more fun while working on our projects. This can be achieved with all the tools, IDEs, text editors, and more, which we use on a daily basis. In this section, we'll take a brief look at popular IDEs and text editors that take advantage of the statically analyzable syntax that Angular provides. We'll also mention the language service that the Angular team developed.

Text editors and IDEs

As we have already said at the beginning of the book, the core team put a lot of effort into enhancing the tooling support in Angular. First of all, the framework is built with TypeScript, which naturally allows us to use static typing during our development process. Some of the text editors and IDEs that have great TypeScript support are as follows:

- **IntelliJ Idea**: A general-purpose IDE by JetBrains.
- **WebStorm**: An IDE specialized for Web development by JetBrains.
- **VSCode**: A cross-platform text editor written in TypeScript and developed by Microsoft.
- **Sublime Text**: A cross-platform text editor.
- **Atom**: A cross-platform text editor written in JavaScript, based on Electron.

Recently, JetBrains announced advanced Angular support in IntelliJ Idea and WebStorm, which supports autocompletion for components and bindings.

Although not all the mentioned IDEs and text editors have Angular-specific features at the time of writing this book, the framework comes with tooling in mind. It allows us to perform advanced static code analysis on the application's code base for the development of sophisticated refactoring and productivity tools in the near future.

Angular language service

Taking advantage of the analyzable nature of Angular, Google developed a **language service** for the framework. We can think of this service as a server, which indexes our project and provides autocompletion suggestions, type checking in templates, based on requests from a client. This client can be a plugin of our text editor or IDE.

The language service can keep track of the context of the given component that is in focus in your text editor and provide context-specific suggestions. For instance, it can provide autocompletion suggestions for directive selectors based on the available set of directives at the given part of the component tree.

The best thing about the language service is that it is not coupled to any specific text editor or IDE, which means that, with a thin plugin, it can be reused in any development environment.

Bootstrapping a project with angular-cli

During AngularConnect 2015, Brad Green and Igor Minar, part of the Angular team, announced `angular-cli`—a **CLI** (**command-line interface**) tool to ease starting and managing Angular applications. For those who have used Ruby on Rails, the idea behind the CLI tool might be familiar. The basic purpose of the tool is to allow the quick setup of new projects and scaffolding of new directives, components, pipes, and services.

At the time of writing, the tool is based on webpack and is in the early stages of development, so we'll demonstrate only its basic usage.

Using angular-cli

In order to install the CLI tool, run the following command on your terminal:

```
$ npm install -g angular-cli
```

Right after this, the `ng` command will appear as global executable in your system. For creating a new Angular project, use the following commands:

```
# May take a while, depending on your Internet connection
$ ng new angular-cli-project
$ cd angular-cli-project
$ ng serve
```

The preceding commands will perform the following:

- Create a new Angular project and install all of its node.js dependencies.
- Enter your project's directory.
- Start a development web server that will let you open the application you have just created in your web browser.

For further reading, take a look at the project's repository, located at `https://github.com/angular/angular-cli`.

Angular quick starters

If you prefer to not get coupled with the CLI tool, there are a lot of starter projects developed by the community that can provide a great starting point for your next Angular project.

Angular Seed

If you enjoy static typing, you can give the **angular-seed** project a try. It is hosted on GitHub at `https://github.com/mgechev/angular-seed`.

The Angular Seed provides the following key features:

- Easy for extend, modular, and statically typed build systems.
- AoT compilation support.
- Supports multiple Angular applications with a shared code base in a single instance of the seed.
- Production and development builds.
- Sample unit tests with Jasmine and Karma.
- End-to-end tests with Protractor.
- A development server with LiveReload.
- Uses codelyzer for static code analysis, which verifies that your project follows the Angular style guide to some extent.
- Follows the best practices for your applications' and files' organization.
- Manager for the TypeScript-related type definitions.
- Provides full Docker support for both development and production environment.

The code distributed with the book is based on this seed project.

For `angular-seed`, you will need to have node.js, npm, and git installed and will need to run the following list of commands:

```
$ git clone --depth 1 https://github.com/mgechev/angular-seed.git
$ cd angular-seed
$ npm install
$ npm start
```

After you have run the preceding commands, your browser will automatically open the home page of the seed. Upon the change of any of the files in your project, the application will be automatically rebuilt, and your browser will be refreshed.

By default, the production build produces a single bundle that contains a minified version of the application and all the referenced libraries. Angular Seed also supports AoT compilation and extensible build systems.

Angular 2 Webpack starter

If you prefer Webpack, you can use *angular2-webpack-starter*. It is a starter project developed by *AngularClass* and hosted on GitHub. You can find it at `https://github.com/AngularClass/angular2-webpack-starter`.

This starter provides the following features:

- The best practices in file and application organization for Angular.
- Ready-to-go build system using Webpack for working with TypeScript.
- Testing Angular code with Jasmine and Karma.
- Coverage with Istanbul and Karma.
- End-to-end Angular code using Protractor.
- Type manager with Typings.

In order to give it a try, you will need to have node.js, npm, and git installed and run the following commands:

```
$ git clone --depth 1
https://github.com/angularclass/angular2-webpack-starter.git
$ cd angular2-webpack-starter
$ npm install
$ npm start
```

AoT compilation in Angular

In this section, we'll briefly explain what AoT compilation is in the context of Angular and what implication it may have on our projects, without going into deep technical details.

The key focus in Angular is it's extremely fast change detection mechanism. After exploring different options for performing change detection, the Angular team discovered that the change detection mechanism used in AngularJS can be improved dramatically using **code generation**. It turns out that generating code, which performs change detection and rendering and on top of that is very well optimized for the JavaScript virtual machine, runs much faster compared to the traditional (also known as dynamic) change detection mechanism.

How code generation works

The Angular code generator is known as the Angular compiler. What it does is compile the templates of the Angular components to JavaScript or TypeScript (depending on the use case). When we compile the templates to TypeScript, we allow the TypeScript compiler to perform type checking, not only within the imperative logic of our components, directives, services and pipes, but also in the components' templates! Performing type checking in the templates helps us find even more potential issues in our application.

On top of code generation for templates, the Angular compiler also generates code for the injectors in our application. This improves the performance of the dependency injection mechanism even further.

Based on the static analysis of the bindings in the templates, the generated code for the templates performs the most efficient change detection and most optimal update of the DOM tree, depending on the changed values. On top of that, the produced code takes advantage of the inline caching mechanism of JavaScript virtual machines, which brings an additional performance boost.

 For further reading about inline caching, take a look at the article *Explaining JavaScript VMs in JavaScript – Inline Caches* located at `http://mrale.ph/blog/2012/06/03/explaining-js-vms-in-js-inline-caches.html`.

The code generation could be either performed at runtime, known as **Just-in-Time** (**JiT**) compilation or build time, known as **Ahead-of-Time** (**AoT**) compilation. Since the JiT compilation involves the evaluation of code at runtime, it is recommended that you use AoT in environments with strict **CSP** (**Content-Security-Policy**), where `eval` is not available.

Introducing AoT compilation

From AoT, we get a couple of improvements. Firstly, if we compile our Angular application as part of the build process, we don't need to compile it at runtime. This has two implications. Firstly, we don't have the runtime performance hit that we get when using JiT. This way, AoT offers faster initial rendering of the application because Angular has to do less work during initialization.

On top of that, since we don't have to perform compilation at runtime anymore, we can drop the entire `@angular/compiler` module out of the final application bundle and decrease the bundle size.

Finally, we can perform much more efficient dead code elimination in terms of **tree-shaking**. Tree-shaking means dropping unused exports, which is one of the great properties of the static nature of the ES2015 modules. When relaying on JiT compilation, we can reference different components by their selectors inside the templates. However, the templates are in HTML-like format, which the modern minifiers (such as uglifyjs, Google Closure Compiler, and so on) don't understand. This means that they cannot eliminate all the unused exports (for instance, unused components), since they are not sure what exactly is used within the templates. Once at build time, the Angular compiler translates the templates to TypeScript or JavaScript, with static ES2015 imports, bundlers can apply traditional dead-code elimination techniques, and so reduce the bundle size even further!

 If you're interested in further reading, you can take a look at the article *Ahead-of-Time Compilation in Angular* at `https://goo.gl/eXieJl`.

Constraints of the AoT compilation

Keep in mind that the Angular compiler needs type metadata in order to perform the process of compilation. This means that you cannot perform AoT compilation if you're not using TypeScript.

AoT compilation is performed without any data collected at runtime. This means that, in some cases, your code may work with JiT but may not work in AoT in case you have dynamic constructs, which cannot be resolved at build time.

For further details, take a look at this repository at `https://goo.gl/F7cV1s`.

Finally, the generated code for the templates is not part of the components' controllers themselves. This means that we cannot bind to non-public fields because, during compilation, TypeScript will throw an error.

How to use the AoT compilation of Angular

The Angular's AoT compilation is already supported in the most popular starters and the CLI.

At the time of writing, Angular CLI does not perform an AoT compilation by default. You can enable it using the `--aot` flag:

```
$ ng build --prod --aot
```

Angular Seed introduced AoT compilation when Angular 2.0.0-rc.5 was released. With the seed, you can take advantage of all the benefits that come with it by performing:

```
$ npm run build.prod.aot
```

By running the commands above, you'll get a well-optimized production build of your application.

Since web tooling changes quite frequently, we didn't go into details of how Angular Seed or Angular CLI produce the production build. If you're interested in further reading on what is going on under the hood, you can take a look at an article at `https://goo.gl/kAiJUJ`.

Summary

We started our journey by introducing the reasons behind the rewrite of Angular, which was followed by a conceptual overview that gave us a general idea about the building blocks that the framework provides. In the next step, we went through a TypeScript crash course that prepared us for `Chapter 4`, *Getting Started with Angular Components and Directives*, where we went deep into Angular's directives, components, and change detection.

In `Chapter 5`, *Dependency Injection in Angular*, we explained the dependency injection mechanism and saw how it's related to the component hierarchy. In the next chapters, we saw how we can build forms and pipes and take advantage of Angular's router.

By completing this chapter, we have finished our journey into the framework. At the time of writing, the design decisions and the ideas behind Angular's core are solid and finalized. Although the framework is still brand new, in the past couple of months, its ecosystem reached a level where we can develop production-ready, high-performance, SEO-friendly applications, and on top of this, have a great development experience with static typing and IDE support.

Index

www.ingramcontent.com/pod-product-compliance
Lightning Source LLC
LaVergne TN
LVHW081338050326
832903LV00024B/1192